Wilderness BRITAIN?

A Greenprint for the Future

DAVID BELLAMY & JANE GIFFORD

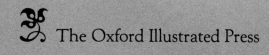
The Oxford Illustrated Press

© 1990. David Bellamy, Jane Gifford

ISBN/85509 225 5

Published by: The Oxford Illustrated Press,
Haynes Publishing Group, Sparkford, Nr Yeovil,
Somerset BA22 7JJ, England

Printed in England by: J. H. Haynes & Co Limited,
Sparkford, Nr Yeovil, Somerset

British Library Cataloguing in Publication Data:
Bellamy, David *1933-*
    Wilderness Britain? : a greenprint for the future.
    1. Great Britain. Environment. Conservation
    I. Title II. Gifford, Jane
    333.720941

    ISBN 1-85509-225-5

Author's Note

So much has been written about wilderness in Britain – but does it really exist? Over the past three years I have explored the more remote parts of Britain in search of land outside our influence. I didn't find any. Instead I entered the fascinating history of the making of the British countryside. The more recent story of its destruction has been well documented. For me, now, the purpose of this book is to show how we can recreate much that we have lost. Taking and researching these photographs has been a great pleasure – if they can help inspire others to save what remains of the traditional British countryside, then they have been worthwhile.

Acknowledgements

Thanks to Joss Pearson, whose initial encouragement helped turn a collection of pictures into an idea for a book, and to Jim Lovelock whose friendship and work have inspired me for the last nine years. Thanks to my mother and Eric for their constant support, and to many friends, especially Rona and Jude. Thanks to David Bellamy and Charles Karsenbarg for their faith in me and for always doing what they promised, and to Oliver Rackham for his wonderful book, *The History of the Countryside,* which was a constant inspiration throughout my research. Thanks for the wealth of information provided by the Nature Conservancy Council, and to John Gaydon and Denise Norman from Ark for their help when things looked bleak. Thanks to David Puttnam, who gave me the confidence to give it a try, and to David Conder from the Council for the Protection of Rural England. Thanks especially to Jane Marshall at Oxford Illustrated Press, who understood when I needed a break.

Above all, thanks to Andrew Lovelock for his infinite patience and constant companionship, for the hours we sat together in the wind and rain waiting for "the perfect moment", and for his enthusiasm, which got me to the top of mountains when my heart was by the open fire in the pub.

Jane Gifford
Summer 1990.

Contents

Foreword

*T*o me the United Kingdom is not made of countryside, punctuated by cities, towns and villages, but is one vast town spreading from coast to coast, with areas of cultivated land and a few parks separating the pseudopods of urban sprawl. It is not so different from other nation states like the Netherlands, Belgium, Denmark and Japan. These national megalopoli share in common abundances of people greater than 1,000 per square mile, most of whom are auto-mobile.

This beautiful and reflective book shows that there is no wilderness left in Britain, nothing of the primeval landscape remains untouched by agriculture, forestry or urban growth. Yet until recently the countryside, although artificial, was a heavenly place where farming and wildlife coexisted, an example to the world that densely populous humans could live in harmony with nature.

Even though agribusiness and urban change have made the land a shadow of the heavenly place it once was, the British Countryside is still worth saving and a fitting subject for Jane Gifford's portraiture. Her photographs and the text she shares with David Bellamy are an optimistic expression of the present countryside. They show that, given the will and the funding, our countryside could return to that state of grace again where we are in harmony with our landscape even though citizens of a town.

Jim Lovelock
Coombe Mill, July 1990

- **97% of all the flower rich meadows GONE**
- **130,000 miles of hedgerow GONE**
- **75% of our internationally important heaths DESTROYED**
- **10 species of dragonflies EXTINCT since the War**
- **Otters MISSING from most of our river systems**
- **All our estuaries CHANGED or THREATENED by pollution, barrages, marinas or other development**
- **The integrity of the Flow Country, one of Europe's last great wild landscapes, DESTROYED by afforestation**

We took it *all* for granted

by David Bellamy

Y ou have probably already looked at all the fabulous photographs. If not take a peep – fantastic aren't they? – that's why, when asked I just had to say yes and be part of this publication.

When I was a small boy, and it wasn't that long ago, a lot more of Britain, even around London where I spent my childhood, looked like the pictures in this book: landscapes overflowing with wildflowers and wildlife, full of beauty and diverse interest right on everybody's back door. From my own home I could get on my bike and cycle through the green lanes of Surrey and Sussex down to the coast at Brighton. En route were well-kept estates and real farms which welcomed you with afternoon tea or even an overnight campsite. All these were set about with small fields and a patchwork of hedges, copses and ponds, all weaning you into the ways of the country, urging you to linger a while longer and to return again and again. Each and every season offered a thousand reasons for making yet another trip.

The same was true over much of these wonderful islands and even the largest towns had unofficial greenspace, complete with frogs and toads and even newts and bats.

It was there, we took it all for granted and now sadly most of it is gone, not I believe as a result of a less caring attitude, but because of the inanities of "progress", pressed upon us by governments, local and national, of every political persuasion and the EEC.

(Consider the sad statistics opposite)

All this destruction and extinction happened despite trojan work by the National Trust, the Wildfowl Trust, the WWF, CPRE, RSPB, RSNC, BTCV, FOE, Greenpeace, the Woodlands Trust and many more. So why, you may well be asking, bother to waste more trees and cause more pollution by helping to publish this book? If it was just another Natural History of Britain picture book – an aren't I clever catalogue of what there has been, to be locked away in the archives of a desolate future – I would have had no part of it. No, this is a hands on, kick up the pants, get off your complacent backsides and do something about it book of ideas and information. And before you read any further, if you are not a member of one or more of these organisations, then join, and if you are then recruit ten more members before it is too late – there's work to do.

At this very moment we are still losing ground, important sites are being destroyed by at least one per cent in each and every year. This must stop. Then there's the real challenge of the "set aside" policy. Thanks in part to the inanities of the common agricultural policy, and the productive success of British farmers, 20% of all our agricultural land is to be taken out of production. Some say that could amount to 12 million acres in the next 25 years. We won't be greedy and will settle for 6 million.

Certainly less than one per cent of that will be

built on, even if planning permission were granted, leaving a staggering area to go back to more natural uses, becoming extensive less intensive farmland held together with coppice woods, water meadows, heathlands, flower-filled pastures, fen, carr, or even bog. A newly accessible greenspace. I like to think of it as the HERITAGE COMMONS holding the rest of our traditional countryside back together; providing corridors and oases of opportunity for our wildflowers and wildlife; buffering the effects of the past and screening the developments of the future, which are crucial to a new economy.

Re-creating wilderness! They must be joking. It's a travesty of terminology, an impossible undertaking. Well with my hand firmly on the heart of the matter and with my ecological training, I can say it's not. When I was a child, no, even sixty generations ago when my ancestors were children, not one rod, pole or perch of Britain was in its truly natural state. It was all people-polluted, people-maintained or people-made. In fact, most of the British countryside that we think of as wild is the result of centuries of human management – heaths, moorland, downland, woodland. That's why we can re-create it all again, and we must do it now.

These pictures you have so enjoyed and will continue to enjoy are not dead records of the past. They have been taken today and they can be living images of the future if only you care enough.

A little bit of prehistory

When people turned up in force for the first time on British soil it was mostly covered with forest and must have been an inhospitable and somewhat boring place. For a start you couldn't have seen the landscape for the trees. Travel would have been a nightmare and the flora and fauna of our native woods, though of interest, is not noted for its great variety.

There would have been some small patches of diversity. Excess rainwater had to drain somewhere and so wetlands, marshes, lakes, fens and bogs would have been features of most catchments. In dry summers, lightning strikes must have sent wild fire raging across the landscape, producing swathes of grassland and heath. But not for long, for the processes of natural succession would soon have healed the damage, covering the land with forest once again.

Eroding river banks, sea-cliffs, mobile shingle, gravel and sand, and rocky outcrops, especially in the mountains, would have provided open ground beyond the reach of the processes of afforestation. These open spaces were of extreme importance, for they acted as living museums for the plants and animals of the pioneer communities which developed as the glaciers of the last ice age went into melt down.

People came to the coastal fringes and estuaries, living on easy pickings of shellfish, fishing rivers and the sea, and hunting the coastal forests. From these home bases, they made their way inland up rivers, choosing the more open spots where they could rest in the comparative safety of a campsite with a view. They developed their technologies of stone which helped them to hunt and gather the richness of their lands – but they had little lasting effect on the landscape, for they lived as part of the wilderness.

Then new migrants brought technologies of farming and of polished stone which could tackle even the toughest trees. With the aid of fire, they started on the job of opening up the forest. New communities of plants – grasslands, heaths, swamps, fens and bogs – and their dependent animals spread out from their natural refugia to take over much larger areas. Open but sheltered communities, drenched in sunlight and full of nectar-rich flowers and succulent herbs, gradually became more widespread and more permanent features of the countryside. Populations of butterflies like the orange-tip, green-veined white, gatekeeper and many more exploded along the woodland edges, while certain bats, small mammals, birds and even reptiles found expanding opportunities in these new more diverse landscapes.

This creative destruction went on apace, aided by bronze and then iron. The first quarries and spoil heaps began to pockmark the countryside, offering the opportunity of bare rock and soil and more open horizons. Some plants and animals benefited from the change, others lost ground. Wolf, bear and wild pig became extinct, just as reindeer, mammoth and giant elk had done before them in the face of the advancing tide of forest and hunting people.

By the time the Romans had conquered Britain, turning the leaves of artifact into the written pages of history, the British scene was set. Changing weather patterns, aiding and aided by the removal of the trees, covered much of our uplands with an expanding blanket of acid peat – 2000 years before the first drops of acid rain fell from a sky stained by industry.

Likewise the lowlands had been opened up into a patchwork of farm, village, field and copse. Even the wildest woods and wetlands were hunted and gathered – so much so that wilderness untouched by dextrous hands and progressive minds ceased to exist. Britain had become a people-made, people-managed place. Yet it was still overflowing with wildlife. And so it was when I was a child, for the creative destruction continued into this sad century, even through the First World War.

Lessons from a history of mismanagement

When I took up my first teaching post at Durham University, set in the industrial northeast of England, I avidly toured the region searching out sites in which I could, with my students, seek excellence in field studies. To my great surprise, I found that many of the sites which were, or later became Sites of Special Scientific Interest (SSSIs) were in fact the floors, faces, margins and spoil heaps of old quarries and mines. Even within that holy of holies, the Upper Teesdale National Nature Reserve, many of the arctic-alpine plants, refugees from the tail-end of the last ice age, were found in abundance on old spoil heaps and mineral enriched talus.

Suddenly it became obvious to me that the ice age had left much of Britain looking not unlike a series of disused quarries and gravel pits, re-mineralized and ready for colonization by any pioneer plants which happened to be carried that way. Natural succession then covered Britain with soil and more stable vegetation, pushing many of the pioneer plants of bare rock and open ground into hiding in small isolated refugia, as forest slowly covered the vast majority of the terrain.

Then along came the agricultural and industrial revolutions which quite by accident put the spice of variety back into the wildlife of the British countryside. That was until the Common Agricultural Policy smothered so much with unwanted cereals and perennial rye-grass, fuelling the idea of production quotas and milking the tax-payers, and creating a new monotony of monoculture soaked with toxic chemicals.

If it hadn't been for the extractive industries, one dreads to think of all that could have been lost from the meagre flora of our counties. To prove it I quote from the official *Macmillans Guide to Britain's Nature Reserves:*

WARDS QUARRY, STAFFORDSHIRE

Permit; 0.3ha; SNCT reserve. Disused quarry. Spring/ summer. The old limestone quarry has been colonised by a flora which includes five species of orchids among over sixty flowering plants.

BLACK PASTURE QUARRY

Permit only; 5 ha; NWT reserve. Large sandstone quarry. Spring/summer. Huge old spoil heaps, thick with oak, ash and sycamore over typical woodland plants, contrast with richer areas with lime-loving plants including quaking grass and fairy flax. More acid open spoil heaps show a sandstone vegetation with scattered scrub of rowan, birch, Scots pine, hawthorn, blackthorn and gorse. Butterflies include red admiral, large skipper and small copper, while among the birds are warblers, finches, woodcock, sparrowhawk and kestrel. The quarry exposes large sandstone beds in the great limestone series, including apple-bedding and fossiliferous horizons.

Yes, until very recently the scars industry left on our landscape were in many regions the only bits of informal greenspace left for nature and local people to enjoy. I, myself, cut my biological teeth in the local brickpits at Cheam in Surrey, long ago tarted up out of all recognition. Sadly the near mania for infilling

holes in the ground with methane-producing rubbish and toxic chemicals has led to the destruction of thousands of these double SSSIs – Sites of Subsidence, Spoil and Industry which later became Sites of Special Scientific Interest. Those we still have left must be saved and we, safe in the knowledge of all that was done by accident in the past, must now look to a new creative future.

We cannot create wilderness but we can put back diversity, so long as we have the local genetic resources from which to work.

Creative quarrying

The sad fact of the matter is that nobody relishes the thought of sharing their back yard with the extractive industries in any shape or form, unless they are a direct beneficiary from the profit. Yet stone and building aggregates are in constant demand and they have to come from somewhere. So until we are willing to pay the increased price, both fiscal and environmental, for long-distance transport, and I mean long, they will have to be found in someone's more local back yard.

Many rightfully argue that with a static or declining population there is in Britain a decreasing need for building material; that with a greening government of whatever political colour going down the right road to public transport there will be less need for roadstone. Be that as it may, we still need to right the wrongs, both past and present, of our acid landscapes. We must remineralise our farms and plantations back towards a more naturally productive future – and to accomplish this our new green lifestyles are still going to need lime and minerals on a massive scale. Holes are going to have to be dug in the ground so we might as well make the most of them.

New creative quarrying and aggregate extraction can and must be based on green gain. In a new "greenprint" economy, faced with the reality of National Parks, Areas of Outstanding Natural Beauty (O.N.B.s), Environmentally Sensitive Areas (E.S.A.s) and set aside, the return of any quarried or opencast land to a prairie landscape is surely wrong, when a diversity of landscape opportunity could result.

Just think of it – new set aside rockscapes for nature conservation, refugia for our mountain and arctic-alpine plants, which are even now under attack in their natural habitats from all that fell-walking and climbing gear. Some quarries can be rockscaped as climbing nurseries for all grades of outward bound endeavour, thus relieving pressure on the natural mountain eyries.

In the same way open water and wetlands can be and are being created – new sanctuaries for wildfowl and wetland plants and animals. (Hooray for the pioneer work of the Wildfowl and Wetlands Trust.)

These can be buffered by areas for fishing, sailing, canoeing, and power-boating – in that descending order of environmental acceptability.

Quarries can hide a lot away both from sight and earshot and, with planning, they can also provide diverse, accessible, even challenging local greenspace. I am not saying that anyone is going to welcome the aggro of mineral extraction in their locale but they should at least be compensated by the end result – greenspace with rights of public access, new (dare I say it) common land.

For those in the waste disposal industry who are saying, "What about our rights of dumpage?", I would point to the wrongs of landfill – groundwater pollution and eutrophication, methane waste and explosions, and the general insult of litter, odour and dust added to the years of injury caused by the digging of the holes in the first place.

I would also point out the recent developments of dealing with our domestic rubbish by recycling, the cogeneration of heat energy and composting. The volume of rubbish we need to dump can thus be reduced by more than 85%, solving many of the problems of landfill caused by straight dumpage. It is clear that the E.E.C. will soon impose penalties for violations of new landfill legislation. Also tax benefits may well accrue from recycling and the reuse of our waste. This would certainly speed up change – so something drastic is going to have to happen. Imagine the whole new technological package – recycling, energy generation and composting – hidden from sight in the deep recesses of our old quarries and gaining local acceptability as it becomes self-financing.

The only problem I can see in all this is that very soon the recycling millionaires will begin to seek out the riches now locked away in old tips. Then local people and their environment will be subject to a third round of extractive abuse and public enquiries will continue to be the dis-order of the day. Even so, starting with our new quarries, the way ahead can and must be through the creation of new greenspace, wildscapes in common ownership.

The new silviculture

The case of woodlands is perhaps the most straightforward of all. Since it is the natural "will" of much of the landscape to revert to forest, all we have to do is help it on its way. We can't recreate real wildwood, but we can plant and manage the next best thing.

At the close of the First World War, Britain was down on its hunkers with only 5% of her landscape covered with trees. The Forestry Commission was set up not to replace our lost native woods but to grow pit props should another war cut off our empire-ical supplies. So the blackwoods came marching across our green and pleasant land, great blocks of alien

monotony, the big green men from Sitka and beyond. At least they were trees and they provided shelter for bluetits, deer and an exploding population of grey squirrels. In time, as these American invaders pushed our native red squirrels north of the border, so some of the old inhabitants of the Caledonian Forest began their push south.

Another World War, a change from Empire to Commonwealth, capped by the E.E.C., made "economic forestry" a clarion call, spurring the need for massive subsidies to make it "economic". Again alien forces began their march across the landscape. In order to profit from economy, the cheapest land suddenly had a subsidised price on its hectarage. More often than not this land was in the last large wild regions in Britain and was home to millions of birds, both resident and migratory, to wildfowl, wildflowers and wildlife. A great diversity of habitats was ploughed up. Highlights in the grand tour for discerning visitors and landscapes which provided sustainable employment for gamekeepers, beaters, ghillies and the tourist infrastructure were swept away under a carpet of conifers.

The new wave forestry began to clear the land of more subtle, more compatible lifestyles, sweeping away traditional countryside professions. They had no voice, for they were small in number, and there are many people who either don't, or don't want to, understand the vital role these old professions play in the management of our wilder places. Profit for the very rich, jobs for a few, and all subsidised by the tax payer. We began to sterilise diversity with monocrop – just as the E.E.C. demanded that much of our farmland be returned from non-economic monocrop to more diverse uses.

I am not against coniferous forestry – both the Commission and the economic forestry groups have become fountains of research, development and action for multiple uses of forest, including habitat creation and conservation. All I am saying, along with the world conservation movement, is that we desperately need new sustainable forests but they must consist of the right trees in the right places. The quicker the zealots of extreme opinion on both sides of the argument bury their chainsaws of disagreement and work together to this end, the better chance there is for the survival of both ourselves and our wildlife.

At least 20%, and I would counsel 25%, of the British Isles should be covered with growing trees by the end of this century. Let's do it now and let's do it right – all those areas of native woodland still left, however tatty their estate, must be conserved. There is no excuse for any more destruction. Each wood is a genetic oasis of what there was, as well as a genetic bank for what there can or must be; each one a treasure-house of local assets and a nucleus for the rebuilding of all our futures.

Thank God we already have the Woodlands Trust who have pioneered the spirit and the practicalities of a new silviculture, encouraging local pride in the

Previous page 15: Open sheep walks and conifer plantations have replaced most of our upland woods. *Previous page 17:* Moorland vegetation has reclaimed a Cornish tin mine. *This page:* Ancient moss-covered oaks on Dartmoor.

ownership and management of local woodlands – woodlands of the community, managed for and by the community, both natural and human.

More recent developments like that in Scotland, styled "Growing up with trees", are life-long, hands on, mud on your boots relationships between youngsters and their local landscape. Under guidance they go out and collect seeds and hardwood cuttings from local stock. They then grow them on to whip stage and beyond in school tree banks, providing local genestock ready to be used in local planting. Gene bank practice and arboriculture in primary schools – of course we are going to win!

Then there are the massive schemes of the

Countryside Commission to plant new urban forests — tens of thousands of acres in the West, the Midlands, and, where else but Sherwood Forest, expanding and joining those areas still under native trees into a stable intermingling of farms and urban sprawl, all contained by woodland.

These are all only ideas now, out to tender, but the optimists, and I am one of them, dream that all and more will be "on stream" in the not too far distant future. And on stream is certainly going to be the operative term, for they will be working woodlands, many earning their keep as coppice.

Coppicing is a practice dating back at least to medieval times. Those native and introduced trees which are amenable actually thrive on massive pruning. Species like hazel, field maple, sweet chestnut, even oak and lime can be harvested at intervals of seven to twenty-two years, again and again on a rotational basis. The managed end result is a patchwork of diversity of native plants and animals and timber products, with soils held firm by ever-present rootstock ("stools" in coppice jargon) and with an annual fall of leaf litter recycling the nutrients. A people-managed working paradise, for there is no doubt, especially in the mind of a botanist, that well-maintained coppice provides more diverse interest than native forest alone.

If we allow ourselves to dream of a million

hectares of working coppice braided across the countryside, then the end result in human, let alone conservation, terms is impressive. Each year these woods would produce 2,000,000 timber trees, firewood equivalent to 5,000 megawatts of energy, half a million tonnes of bark and chemical-rich wood waste, and 12,000 direct jobs in coppice and coppice management. The majority of these jobs would be in the more rural areas, offering a direct link between town and country during the main work periods, when a large holiday workforce will also be required.

These areas of coppice would ideally form buffers between and around the wildwood reserves and the new production forests of fast-growing conifers – yes, there must be a place for conifers in the economy of our new countryside, for without them it would be impossible to balance (let alone make) the books of import and export. At the moment our timber and wood pulp imports stand second only to food.

When planted along the contours in landscape harmony, ugly blocks of conifers can be transformed into landscape features. Planned and planted with buffer fans and ribbons of native broadleaf trees along watercourses, they take on a whole new conservation dimension. Conifer plantations can be tailored to produce a coppice-like patchwork with adjacent stands of a range of ages providing a diversity of habitat, both in space and time, and opportunities for birds like the crossbill, goshawk, siskin and short-eared owl and for animals like deer, pine martin, badger and fox.

Access roads for logging and fire protection can serve the same functions, acting also as routes for visitors on foot, bicycle and horseback, becoming sunlit rides full of butterflies and moths. If hardcored with limestone and dolomite, these same tracks provide habitats for a whole range of lime-loving plants and animals, as well as acting as buffers against increasing acidity – a function not only of acid rain but also of habitat abuse.

The removal of a crop of trees also takes with it part of nature's own local supply of minerals, including those which combat acidity. If these are not replaced by recycling and continued soil formation, then acidification will inevitably follow. Grow any crop after crop, especially in the wetter West, and acid soil must result, even in the absence of acid rain.

To prove the point, when neolithic farmers first arrived upon the scene, the British Isles and much of Ireland was covered with forest. Replacement of the trees with grazing animals and with crops was brought about through many cycles of slash and burn. With nothing being put back in return, vast areas of land across central and western Ireland and Scotland, and on the hills of western England and Wales turned sour. A wetter climate helped the process on, covering once wooded landscapes with a blanket of acid peat. So it was that our acid moorlands, wet heaths and bogs came into being long before acid rain was even thought of.

Mountains and moorlands

*T*oday our mountains and moorlands, our wildest and most uninhabited places, are under massive attack by coniferisation and by the boots and tyres of off-road walkers and cyclists. The habitats of our upland birds and plants are being smothered with conifers or loved to death by visitors. Both have got to stop or at least the causes must be managed in the right way. The heights and slopes of our uplands and broad expanses of blanket bog and heath are not the best places in which to practice agroforestry. The lower peat-free, now very marginal farmland (which should be moving into set aside) has a more amenable climate and is mainly already roaded. Surely this is where the new trees would grow best and who better to benefit from planting and management grants than the tenant farmers and crofters?

Wherever trees are planted, open vistas should be left at all points along road and rail routes. Like their neolithic forebears, visitors come to appreciate the view. They come to see the fells, not the felled trees. With the trees lower down, the uplands can be left for golden eagles, merlin, peregrine falcons, grouse and deer. I apologise in advance to all those who decry blood sports, for so do I, but the sad fact is that the deer population must be contained, for if they are allowed to breed unchecked then the natural processes of soil protection and succession will stop, wildwood will disappear and the soil and peat will erode away. Management of some sort is now essential.

We can either decry blood sports out of hand or thank our lucky stars that there are people who appear to enjoy doing the job of culling wildlife and who are willing to pay for the privilege. Deer forests and grouse moors will always be littered with bones of contention, especially for vegetarians. For those who eat meat, and even those who don't, please ask yourselves which causes most stress to the animals concerned – a lamb raised on the open fells and then loaded into a truck for a long fearful journey to the abattoir, or a deer quietly grazing and then bang it's dead? Chickens raised in deep litter or free range (I won't even mention the obscenities of battery farming) gathered up and slaughtered, or birds living free in their own habitat until the Inglorious Twelfth?

Perhaps the saddest reflection of all is that, even if we all became vegetarians, deer along with the other so-called vermin of the fells would still have to be culled. By whom? People from the ministry, using tax payers' money, hired guns and poison? Moreover, if we remove the "cruel" economy of hunting, shooting and fishing, conifers will take their place and a new sort of slaughter will begin all over again. There is, as far as I can see, no rational answer. We have altered the balance of our landscape, creating diversity from the original uniformity of wildwood, so now we must bear the responsibilities of management.

Top: The Lakeland
Fells, suffering under
the pressure of their
accessibility.
Above: Beyond the
tree limit on the
Torridon mountains.
Left: Applecross,
remote and impassable
in winter but long ago
deforested.

Wild water and wetlands

*F*ollowing the acidified water from upland catchments down to the sea, we pass through the problems and potentialities of our wetlands. In the days of natural Britain, wetlands provided the main pools of diversity in an otherwise silvine landscape. Yet the trees were always there, waiting their chance to swallow up the water.

With the removal of the trees, acid bog became the dominant landform across vast areas and remained so until drainage and afforestation took their massive toll. The recent and continuing destruction of so much of the Flow Country of Caithness and Sutherland, one of Europe's last great wild regions, will forever blot our conservational copy book.

The main areas of lowland bog in England, Wales and southern Scotland have suffered too, drained and cut for peat which is used for a variety of purposes from electricity generation to potting compost. The mass annihilation of the peatlands of Ireland is another of the saddest acts of this sad century. Action must be taken immediately.

Areas of bog still in a near pristine state must be protected in reserves – for they are the last few per cent of our unique boglands. As the winning of peat from areas already mutilated by drainage and cutting comes to an economic end, some of the profits from the last cuts must be used for rehabilitation. There is ample evidence that the older methods of commercial peat extraction left cutaways which, when flooded, provided a habitat for much of the original flora and fauna. If planned in the right way whilst the machinery is still on site, regeneration can be set in motion on a vast scale. This is now the only hope over large areas.

Fens, marshes and watermeadows are much easier to recreate, as long as the genestock is available and the water supply is not too polluted and over-enriched with nutrients. The East Anglian broads and fens are perfect examples of the creative power of people. The Broads are no more or less than areas from which peat was cut for fuel way back in medieval times. If they could create the basis for what is now a multi-million pound tourist industry and a National Park, using no more than spades and shovels, just think what could be accomplished with a J.C.B.

I look with creative desire at the potential of some of the fenland farms, now reduced to set aside status. A new crop of broads and linking dykes, some with tiny villages and waterborne pastimes, others purely for wildflowers, wildfowl and wildlife. Let's create another Broadland National Park and provide the peat industry with a new creative purpose in its declining years.

Fens were but ribbons of open green along the rivers until the harvesting of reeds for thatch, osiers for basket-making and sedge for animal litter pushed back the trees and opened the land. What is more, it has now been shown that fen and swamp vegetation

can soak up excess nutrients draining from the land and combat certain types of pollution. Wetlands can play a new-part in the economy of our water resource.

Likewise watermeadows, now sadly all but destroyed, can be reinstated. They too have a role to play in set aside and environmentally sensitive farming, being a living filter between the excesses of the land and the purity of our flowing waters. Along our rivers the fishing fraternity must continue to play their all-important role as the eyes, ears and voice of the waterways. They are our wardens and watchdogs, checking out the signs of change and pushing legislation ever onwards towards cleaning up our water act. Now with their acceptance of lead-free weights and their on-bank training of the next generation of environmentalists, their presence along our waterways still bodes good, except for the unlucky fish that didn't get away.

The fish that do get away and try to return to the sea to complete their life cycles still have the problem of our estuarine and inshore waters to contend with. Problems which have made many of our so-called bathing beaches unfit even for paddling. Long sea outfalls discharging raw sewage out of sight are not the answers to the problem.

Living Farmscapes

*L*ast, but by no means least, we come to our farmscapes – grass and croplands once again beset with hedge and woodlots. I never did understand why hedges were torn down, opening up the soil to massive wind damage, drying and erosion. Enlarging the farm gates to accommodate the combines would surely have made as much productive sense. Many farmers and farm workers, the few that are now left on the land, bemoan the loss of landscape privacy and the legacy of pheasant and partridge, and wildflowers for the church and the W.I.

Our hedges, some dating back to Saxon times, were torn down. They can be replanted, complete with well spaced trees, although the cost is high. Research has shown that if the headlands (awkward bits of fields) are left unploughed and unplanted and the softer, biodegradable, slow-release, targeted agrichemicals are used on the land, then the full diversity of farm wildlife soon returns.

Wire-to-wire fitted perennial rye grass may well be productive in terms of supergrass, but it uses up an awful lot of expensive nitrogen. With quotas now limiting the production of milk, cows may once again be economically grazed (and research has shown more contentedly) on flower-filled pastures. Moreover, with meadows filled with flowers producing a surfeit of sweet-scented hay, our rivers and water supplies will be less prone to enrichment by nitrates.

One of the great developments of recent years has been the replacement of well-mown lawns in parks, gardens and even roadside verges by mini-meadows.

Previous page 23: A lone tree, the first of many that will eventually swallow up this reed-filled pool in the natural process of succession.
This page: Apple blossom. Many old orchards have been uprooted to make way for fields of grain, motorways and housing estates.

This has not only given our wildflowers and insects their last chance of survival in vast areas of our chemical-drenched landscapes, but has in places drastically reduced the on-going costs of amenity management. With at least one million acres of urban gardens ready to grow green, multi mini-meadows and native shrubberies may soon be ripe with a harvest of flowers, fruits, nuts and insects, each in due season.

Farm ponds, too, are coming back into fashion, not to service farm animals and tractors, but as features of new multi-purpose farmscapes in which visitors are as commonplace as our once-rare breeds. What is more, the general public are beginning to

demand healthy food and conservational grade farming, mixing the best of the old with the best of the new, and true organic husbandry is beginning to help meet the demands of our green shoppers.

Our downlands and lowland heath, made famous by Charles Darwin, Hardy and Elliot and many more, are another case in question. Always of marginal farming importance, they should never have been put to the plough. It was a total waste of time, effort and tax payers' money. They, too, should be returned to their former flowerful glory. Likewise the urban and conifer sprawl, which in places threatens the last remaining remnants of heath (including S.S.S.I.s and local nature reserves) must be stopped. In the meantime we must start to put it all back into working order.

To put Britain back into its flower, bird, animal and insect filled technicolour glory and to manage it into perpetuity is the goal — and it's going to cost a lot of money and continued effort. The money is there through set aside, E.S.A. and A.O.N.B. grants and the like, and through the new economic multiple use of our landscapes. So, too, is the effort and expertise thanks to the membership and workforce of organisations like the National Trust, the C.P.R.E., the B.T.C.V., the R.S.P.B. and the R.S.N.C. A new coactive link between town and countryside — whether we succeed . . . is up to you.

oes true wilderness still survive on these overcrowded islands? If we define wilderness as land outside our influence, then the answer is a definite no. Four thousand years of human exploitation have changed even our remotest countryside — the Scottish Highlands, the mountains of Snowdonia, Dartmoor, the mudflats of East Anglia, the saltmarshes and fenlands of Norfolk, even our cliffs and beaches. Today agri-business, commercial forestry, industry, fish-farming, urban development, road-building and tourism threaten the destruction of the last fragments of Britain's ancient countryside.

Our influence on the land is far-reaching. Even the remotest corners of Britain are in some way an expression of a partnership between mankind and the land. Centuries of labour have created a beautiful, diverse and self-sustaining "working environment"; a landscape that worked both for us and with us. The British countryside is a living social document; a record of past attitudes towards life and the land.

In the last fifty years there has been a dramatic change in our relationship with the countryside. Traditional cyclical methods of managing our resources, which took advantage of nature's powers of regeneration and which put back into the land much that was taken out, have been abandoned. Plant communities deriving from hundreds, sometimes thousands, of years of consistent human management are now threatened with extinction.

We have become increasingly dependent upon systems of farming and forestry and supplies of energy which rely heavily on finite resources, particularly fossil fuels. Even the nitrogenous chemical fertilisers, on which modern agriculture and forestry depend are derived from oil. Intensive methods of production are unworkable without pesticides. Dependent upon ever-increasing doses of chemicals, this system is

unsustainable. Gardeners, too, rely on a huge variety of poisons. In 1985 alone, we spent over thirty million pounds on garden pesticides and weed killers.

Genetic engineering – the "manufacturing" of plants and animals funded mainly by the chemical industry — is now seen as the answer to current problems. Scientific journals are already full of reports of alien introductions decimating indigenous wildlife; flatworms from New Zealand are wiping out native earth worms in Northern Ireland. The cane toad, introduced to Australia 50 years ago to control a beetle that was destroying sugar crops, is now such a pest that scientists are considering introducing a virus

Wilderness Britain?

A greenprint for the future

by Jane Gifford

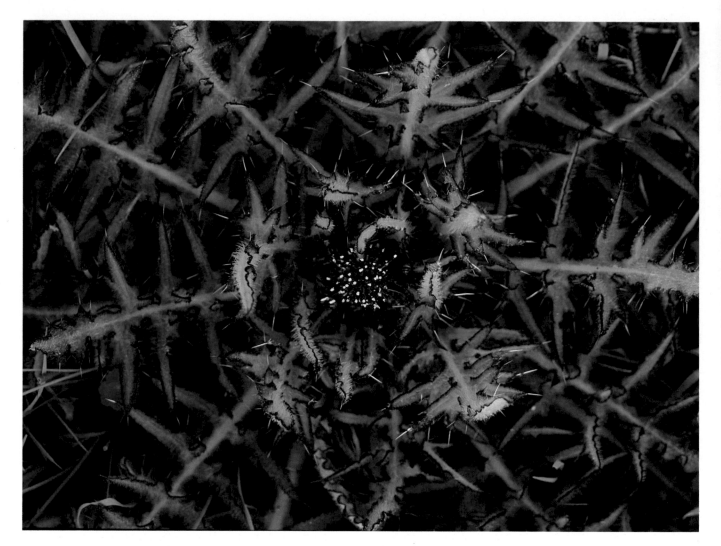

or bacterium to control it. Hawaii's native vegetation is being devastated by the faya tree, introduced by immigrant labourers in the 1920s.

What price will our native vegetation pay for the release of genetically manipulated organisms into the environment? The accidental introduction of an American saltmarsh grass produced a vigorous hybrid which is now colonising Britain's coastal marshes to the exclusion of all other plantlife. The government have opted for secrecy on genetic engineering to avoid unfair commercial competition. The public will not be informed about releases.

Intensive farming, especially in cereal production, is costing us the soil itself. We are well aware of the problems of flash-flooding and soil erosion associated with the destruction of the rainforests. Graphic television pictures of dust bowls in North America and Australia, deserts in the making as a result of over-intensive agriculture and grazing, have shocked us all. But we are not learning from mistakes elsewhere — soil erosion is now becoming a widespread and serious problem in Britain. We continue to regard the earth, like so much else, as a disposable commodity, while, at the same time, producing vast quantities of hazardous

waste — toxic chemicals and radioactive compounds. If the landscape is a reflection of our life-style, what will we leave behind for our children?

The effectiveness of popular pressure

*T*he strength of popular concern for our own health and, more recently, for the health of the environment is indicated by the enormous success of publications like *E for Additives* and *The Green Consumer Guide.*

■ Friends of the Earth's campaign to draw public attention to the connection between ozone depletion and the use of CFCs in aerosol cans prompted British manufacturers to switch to "ozone friendly" spray cans.

■ Greenpeace have forced governments, and particularly the cosmetic industry, to remove their support from the whaling industry.

■ Lynx, the anti-vivisection lobby, and Anita Roddick of the Body Shop have forced a move away from products which involve cruelty to animals.

■ Pop stars like Bob Geldof and Sting, and comedians like Lenny Henry and Ben Elton have focused our attention on the problems of the Third World and the consequences of rainforest destruction. They have shown how much we can achieve by sheer strength of numbers. Millions of pounds have been raised by public donation.

Creative consumption is our most effective means of changing the attitudes of government and industry in favour of the environment. There are too many vested interests for changes in the present system to be made without our personal commitment and encouragement. There are now many publications helping us to make choices about the food we eat, about cleaning products, fuels, toiletries and consumer goods which minimise harm to the environment. The onus is on the individual to become well-informed. There is a list of organisations both happy to help and in need of your support, at the back of this book.

- Consider the cost to the environment of the manufacture, use and disposal of goods.
- Consume less, buy second hand and repair things.
- Avoid over-packaged products and those derived from threatened species and habitats, and favour reusable packaging.
- Favour recycled goods *and* make sure your own rubbish – glass, paper and tin cans – is recycled. Insist upon an informative and standardised system of labelling *and* make a habit of reading the information provided.
- When comparing the price of produce from organic and intensive farms, remember that the price of non-organic produce is kept artificially low by a massive amount of public subsidy.
- Remember, too, that the ploughing up and fencing off of common land on heaths, downs, moors and woodlands throughout Britain has been funded by tax payers' money. The public have paid to be excluded from more of the countryside than ever before.

Industrialists and politicians are currently falling over themselves to stress their concern for environmental issues. But let's consider a few facts:

- Britain continues to dump chemical waste and untreated sewage sludge in the North Sea despite fierce opposition from other EEC countries and despite a recent survey of 20,000 flatfish in the North Sea which showed forty per cent to be deformed.
- Britain has so far refused to accept that the seabed of the North Sea is an unsuitable place to dump nuclear waste.
- Around 300 million gallons of sewage are discharged into the sea around Britain every day. "Sewage sickness" is now common amongst bathers in contaminated water.
- The European Commission will prosecute Britain over three of its most polluted beaches including Blackpool, the country's most popular resort, unless the situation quickly improves.
- The build up of toxic blue-green algae in our over-enriched waters has forced the Department of Health to issue a warning not to eat shellfish and crustaceans from the northeast coast.
- Britain is the largest producer of sulphur dioxide pollution (a major cause of acid rain) in Western Europe. In the run up to privatisation of the electricity industry, the government has cut by thirty per cent, plans to fit coal-fired power stations with desulphurisation equipment.
- Large amounts of sulphur from acid rain are accumulating in the soils of our remotest countryside. Fish populations in our lakes and rivers are falling dramatically as a result of over-acidification of the water.
- Britain has over 4,000 landfill sites taking domestic and industrial waste. A recent survey for the Department of the Environment found that 62% had no means of monitoring ground water pollution and 70% had no control over the build-up of explosive gases.
- A Bristol company developed a system to reprocess organic refuse producing compost, fibre board and solid fuel. The plant is driven by gases produced in the process. Council authorities have refused to take up the idea.
- Carbon dioxide, produced by burning fossil fuels, especially in cars and power stations, is a major greenhouse gas contributing to the problems of global warming. Current massive investment in roads rather than public transport adds to the problem.
- Planned new roads threaten the survival of no less than 155 Sites of Special Scientific Interest. A government spokesman recently explained that if SSSIs had been guaranteed absolute protection then he could assure the public that very few would ever have been set up!

*T*he following pages show how our past involvement with the land has created much that is worthwhile and beautiful, and remind us of what we will lose if we fail to recognise our responsibility towards the environment. Most of us are well-intentioned, but there is still an element of hypocrisy. How can we consider ourselves a nation of animal lovers when the RSPCA has to destroy 2,000 dogs a day? Why do we accept the appalling conditions in which most of our livestock are kept, especially pigs and poultry, on factory farms today? The fate of the British countryside is in our hands. Our attitude towards it and the positive contribution we make towards its conservation are of fundamental importance to the future quality of life, both here and throughout the world. JG

I cut my conservational teeth in coppice woodland management. Sounds very grand doesn't it? Real Capability Bellamy stuff. In actual fact it was while a member of the 1st Belmont Boy Scout Troop. We paid for our campsite on the Weald in Surrey by helping the farmer with his work in his coppice woods.

Yes, less than 50 years ago coppice woodlands still played an important part in the economy of the farmscapes even of the stockbroker belt. They provided smallwood for fuel and for the handles of tools, and wattle for hurdles and the reinforcement of streambanks. The standard trees – oak, elm, and even wild service – still stood twelve and more to the acre and when felled they provided good sound timber for

a variety of purposes on the estate.

These working woodlands also provided a successional matrix of ever-changing habitats; airy and flooded with sunlight in the years after coppicing, then gradually getting more and more shaded and humid as the coppice stools grew their crop of straight, strong poles.

There was always kindling wood in plenty and a changing panoply of wild flowers; primroses (I could always pick a bunch for my mum's birthday), early purple orchids, yellow archangel, woodspurge, bugle and, if you knew where to look, herb Paris, and fragrant daphne. Wild strawberries were there for the picking, amidst the constant flit of butterflies, songs of birds and the staccato of the yaffle, woodpecking

Working Woodlands

his woodland way of life.

It was hard work and we always slept well, after listening to the stories of the gamekeeper, fragrant woodsmoke drifting into the tents. He explained how coppicing had provided energy for the ironmasters of the past, fuelling the first steps of the industrial revolution. He showed us the hammer ponds, once part of industry and now part of the diversity of greenscape, providing fishing grounds for otters. He showed us the abundance of hazel nuts and honeysuckle which helped fill his woodland with fragrance, making it a fitting home for the shy dormouse. Above all, he made us understand that death was part of the living cycle and that he had an important job to do in keeping down vermin – which

in his book included stoats, weasels, rats and even roe deer.

I marvelled at the knowledge of the man and the gentle nature of someone who had to be a part of killing in his profession. Why is it that "gamekeeper" has connotations of cruelty, while "shepherd" those of pastoral care? I will never understand how people can find pleasure at the shooting party, but I do understand the role of our coppice woodlands, both to conservation and to the economy of the countryside.

Our coppice woodlands must be put back into working order, and on a massive scale. Sadly, many must pay their way with game – at least until those who say no find the will and the way to make them economical, working woodlands once more. DB

Right: The Forest of Dean rises like rainforest above early morning mist over the Wye Valley. Similar broadleaf woodland once covered most of the British Isles.

Far right: 4,500 years ago the Caledonian wildwood extended over mountain slope and misty glen throughout Scotland. The Scots pine had its stronghold in the central Highlands.

Britain was once a densely forested land. 4,500 years ago broadleaf woodland covered most of the country except the central Highlands where the Scot's pine flourished. Birch was commonest in the far north of Scotland. Oak and hazel woodland grew on the moors of Cornwall and Devon and on the Welsh and English hills. Lime woods extended across most of lowland England, while elms were mostly confined to the southwest corner of Wales.

Britain's native woods have a remarkable capacity for self-renewal. Land cleared by early settlers soon reverted to woodland when left untended. Our trees are not easily killed. When burnt or felled they shoot again from the roots or the stump. Long ago we learnt to take advantage of this capacity for regeneration.

A walkway of oak planks was recently discovered preserved in peat on the Somerset Levels. Poles from 6 different species of tree had been used to make the supporting stakes and hurdles and each type of wood served a separate and distinctive purpose. Dating back to 3900BC, the "Sweet Track", as it is known, is the earliest evidence we have of woodmanship in Britain.

As villages became centres of settled agriculture, so the pace of forest clearance quickened. Grazing animals and regular burning prevented the natural regeneration of trees and the wildwood gradually receded. Today only isolated pockets of broadleaf forest remain – islands of the past in a sea of arable and pasture land.

The management of woodland as a sustainable resource. *Above left:* A pollarded beech on the Mendips. The branches are cut above the reach of grazing animals, leaving a permanent trunk which sprouts anew after each harvest.

As trees were removed from the British landscape, so those that remained became more valuable and systems of management were developed to preserve woodland as a self-sustaining resource. In "coppiced" woods, trees were felled at regular intervals and allowed to regrow from the stump, the new growth supplying wood for fencing, hurdles, baskets, tools and bindings as well as fuel for furnaces and domestic use. Coppicing actually prolongs the natural life of trees. Coppice stools that are over 1000 years old are still producing good crops of poles today.

In woodland used as common pasture trees were protected from grazing animals by being "pollarded". Each tree was cut to a height beyond the animals' reach, leaving a permanent trunk which sprouted in the same way as a coppice stool. Under both systems of management – coppicing and pollarding – some trees, particularly oaks, were left untouched until full-grown and then felled for timber. By the eleventh century most broadleaf woodland was under some form of management, although links with the original wildwood remained.

Above: A coppiced beechwood in Gloucestershire. The trees are felled every 15-50 years, leaving a permanent stump which will continue to produce crops of straight, strong poles almost indefinitely.

The dense displays of spring flowers so characteristic of Britain's native woods are partly the result of past management. Plants like primroses, wood anemones and bluebells can tolerate shade, but it isn't essential. When pollarding and coppicing open up the woodland canopy, these flowers flourish and multiply with the increase in sunlight. As the trees grow back, the wood again becomes darker. Tall grasses, intolerant of shade, are suppressed and prevented from smothering low-growing plants. This cycle of light and dark years accompanying management encourages a continuous carpet of woodland flowers. Deer are not partial to bluebells and their selective grazing often allows them to flower in extraordinary numbers. When management ceases, this colourful herald of spring soon fades.

Continued reliance on natural regeneration to fill clearings in Britain's oldest woodland has left a fragile link with the plant communities of the prehistoric wildwood. The lime tree, Tilia cordata, and flowers like ramsons, herb-Paris and oxlips seem only to thrive on sites that have always been wooded. They are useful indicators of antiquity. The management of native woodland has now largely been abandoned in Britain and in the past 40 years over a third of our ancient coppices have tragically been grubbed up for agriculture or replanted with conifers; of our native trees only the pine does not respond to either coppicing or pollarding. Each wood destroyed was a unique and irreplaceable record of the past, and a sustainable source of future energy and timber.

Left: Bluebells in a
Wiltshire wood: dense
displays of spring
flowers are
characteristic of our
ancient woods. Well
maintained coppice
provides more diverse
wildlife interest than
native woodland alone.

Above: Herb Paris
(*Paris quadrifolia*)
seems only to thrive in
our oldest woods and
is a useful indicator of
antiquity.
Left. The massed white
flowers of garlic-
scented ramsons
(*Allium ursinum*) also
indicate long-
established woodland.

Left: Scots pines on the lower slopes of the Cairngorms. There is no sign of new growth below the trees. Tender saplings are soon browsed by hungry deer, whose numbers are rapidly rising in the absence of any natural predator.

*I*n the Scots pinewoods of northern Britain there is a deceptive air of constancy. Once pine and birchwoods covered the Scottish Highlands. Today less than one per cent of this natural woodland remains. A wetter trend in the climate, peat formation, burning, grazing and deliberate clearance have had a devastating effect on the northern forestlands. Only isolated fragments have survived. Even their isolation makes them vulnerable – if any plant species dies out, there is nowhere nearby to provide seeds for recolonisation.

In a few places like Abernethy and Beinn Eighe there has probably been a continuous cover of woodland for the past 8000 years. Plant communities here are a last direct link with the flora of the Caledonian wildwood. The most striking aspect of these ancient woods is their diversity. Unlike the dense monocultures typical of modern plantation forestry, natural pine woodland is relatively open and liberally sprinkled with other species of tree. Birch, rowan, bird cherry and wood hawthorn prosper amongst the Scots pines, with willow and alder favouring waterlogged ground.

On the woodland floor a rich variety of mosses and lichens are woven into a continuous springy carpet. Bilberry, cowberry, heather and juniper form a fragrant shrubby understorey where young ferns uncoil in the moist shelter of the trees. Orchids such as autumn lady's – tresses bloom in plenty and the delicate white flowers of wintergreen chickweed still open in summer. Many insects, including over 40 species of beetle, depend on ancient pinewoods for their survival.

Above and below: Rothiemurchus Forest, Britain's largest remaining tract of ancient pinewood. As much a part of our national heritage as castles and stately homes, the integrity of the forest is slowly being destroyed by planting it with foreign conifers.

Right: Fly agaric (*Amanita muscaria*) is always associated with birchwoods. The toadstools appear as the autumn leaves begin to turn.

Below: In Britain's northern birchwoods, the rocks, bark and the earth itself are covered with lichens – a fragile miniature jungle and a sensitive monitor of air pollution.

The birch was one of the first trees to recolonise Britain after the last ice age. A tree of the arctic tundra, it thrives in the Scottish Highlands. Birchwoods satisfied many of our basic needs. As well as providing fuel, the bark was used for tanning leather and making charcoal, and cut for slats and shingles. Small branches were bound together to make fire beaters and besoms, or plaited into tough cords for binding rafts of pine logs. Wood was used for kitchen implements, barrel staves and furniture. Even the sap was used to make wine. 150 years ago there was still an active birch economy in northern Britain. Today our birchwoods are an undervalued and neglected resource.

Fly agaric, the popular fairy toadstool with its spotted scarlet crown and frilly white skirts, is closely associated with birch woods. Fungi like the strangely greasy Scarlet hood and members of the lycoperdon family, like pear-shaped sea urchins, can also be found growing on the mossy turf. Many species of woodland fungus still abundant in continental Europe, are becoming rarer in Britain as a result of habitat destruction. Unscrupulous pickers increase the risk of extinction.

Away from major industrial centres, a fragile miniature jungle covers the trees and mossy banks of Britain's woods. In shades of green, blue and silver, dotted with scarlet, these strange plants are lichens. They are the result of a close symbiotic relationship between two separate organisms – a fungus makes up the body of the lichen within which single-celled algae provide the nutrients essential for the life of both. Lacy and frond-like, brittle and sponge-like, lichen communities once grew on trees throughout the British Isles.

Lichens are nature's monitor of air pollution.

They are particularly sensitive to contamination by
sulphur dioxide – a by-product of burning fossil
fuels (coal, gas, oil and petrol) and a major cause
of acid rain. This is the main reason for their
disappearance throughout the industrial lowlands.
The varying resistance of different species to
contamination allows us to map pollution levels
throughout the country. One greenish-yellow
granular lichen, *Lecanora conizaeoides*, only grows
where the air is polluted. Unknown in Europe
before 1860, it has since become abundant in
Britain and throughout the northern continent.

Surrounded by a rising
sea of Norway and
Sitka spruce, the
birchwoods of
Glenfeshie have been
reduced to a few
fragments along the
river. 150 years ago the
birch tree satisfied
many basic needs.

It is unclear how far the decline of Britain's upland woods can be attributed to acid rain, although it is certainly a contributing factor. In many places foliage is noticeably thinning. The threat posed by intensive grazing, however, is inescapable. The red deer and the roe deer have lived amongst the trees of the Scottish Highlands for thousands of years. We have long since exterminated their natural predators, the wolf, the bear and the lynx, and today there are estimated to be around twice as many deer in Scotland as the land can support. Deer stalking is a valuable source of income to many estates and unscrupulous owners have a vested interest in keeping herd

Clear-felled slopes and solitary pines are often all that remains of Scotland's native pinewoods. Where the trees remain, over-grazing by sheep and deer prevents natural regeneration, contributing to the final demise of our highland woods.

numbers artificially high. Starving deer are now a common sight in severe winters.

Our upland woods are struggling to survive under extreme grazing pressure. Where once there was a range of trees of all ages, there is now little sign of new growth. Deer strip the bark and eat the growing shoots of young trees. Sheep crop seedlings close to the ground, while cattle trample the delicate flora. If we don't invest in livestock fencing or substantially reduce stocking levels, Britain's upland woods will be increasingly confined to inaccessible crags beyond the reach of grazing animals and outside the bleak confines of commercial pine plantations.

Above: Damp hollows below the Scots pines of Beinn Eighe are lined with a rich mixture of ferns, mosses and liverworts. The most striking aspect of these ancient woods is their diversity.

Right: Coille na Glas Leitire has a wooded history stretching back 8,000 years. Such ancient woodland provides an invaluable link with the plant communities of the prehistoric wildwood.

Britain's first National Nature Reserve was established at Beinn Eighe in 1951, principally to conserve a fragment of ancient Caledonian pinewood – called Coille na Glas Leitire – growing on the shores of Loch Maree. Most of the Scots pines between 80 and 200 years old had already been felled in the 1940s but fortunately some of the older, less manageable trees were left standing. The excellent timber was mainly used to make cartridge boxes. Woodland recovery has proved to be a slow process. It has taken over 40 years for saplings to develop on the cleared ground.

Successful regeneration of pines on the Reserve requires a certain amount of luck and careful management. A good seed-producing year has to coincide with the right conditions for germination. This might happen as seldom as once in 20 years. Before most of the wood was felled, fire due to lightning damage was an important part of woodland ecology, clearing away excessive scrub and providing a fertile seed bed for future generations of trees. Coille na Glas Leitire is probably too small and too isolated to retain all of its characteristic plants if it burns today. Fire is now a constant threat to its survival.

To help prevent disaster many young trees, grown only from local seed, have been planted in deer-proof enclosures on surrounding land, where certain plants like bilberry and cowberry indicate the former presence of woodland. A controlled cull of deer is carried out each year to limit browsing on the rest of the reserve and to improve the chances of natural woodland regeneration. The remaining deer are healthier as a result. Trees are regularly measured and photographed to provide a reliable record of growth. This is essential to the assessment of management policies.

Wardens and conservation volunteers have worked hard to maintain excellent nature trails and to provide information for visitors. In 1976, the United Nations Educational Scientific and Cultural Organisation (UNESCO) designated Beinn Eighe a Biosphere Reserve in recognition of its international importance. In 1983 the Reserve was awarded a European Diploma by the Council of Europe.

Beinn Eighe National Nature Reserve is now part of an international network dedicated to the conservation of nature and scientific research.

Wistman's Wood: mossy dwarf oaks on high boulder-strewn moorland. A last remnant of Dartmoor's prehistoric tree-cover. Oaks grew on high ground throughout England and Wales before the advent of human clearance.

Right: Hanging oak woodland in the Elan valley.

Far right: Longleat Estate. Oaks were once confined to areas with poor soils. Traditionally Britain's most important timber trees, oaks have since been planted in woodland, on pasture, and in parks and gardens throughout the country.

*I*n their natural habitat oakwoods are typical of regions with thin infertile soils. A good example is Wistman's Wood. Huddled on the steep slopes of a remote Dartmoor valley, it is a powerful and mysterious place. Its squat, ancient oaks are covered in mosses, lichens, ferns and sedges. A small part of the wood has been protected from livestock and the public since the sixties. In this part a thicket of young trees and brambles has appeared, in sharp contrast to the surrounding open woodland, where the undergrowth is sparse.

For thousands of years we have favoured oaks as our most important timber trees and they are no longer confined to regions with poor soils. Oaks were easily grown into the curved shapes necessary for the cruck frames of houses and the hulls of ships. The strong durable timber provided beams for the roofs of cathedrals and castles and a host of other purposes. Demands from the navy in the 16th century led to the widespread planting of oakwoodland. Planting has continued down the centuries and tall oak trees are now a feature of woods throughout the country and of hedgerows, parks and gardens everywhere.

It is a popular myth that most of our oakwoods were destroyed during the Industrial Revolution. In fact this association with industry has saved many ancient woods from clearance. Conversion to agricultural land and plantation forestry has caused far greater losses. Surviving oakwoods on the Welsh and English hills would probably have been cleared for sheep if they had not provided charcoal for furnaces. The Forest of Dean has been a major industrial centre since the Roman's first plundered its iron ore. Nineteenth century foresters did more harm to woodland ecology here than centuries of industry. They exterminated the indigenous oaks and planted a "superior" species of oak which later proved far less successful than the original trees.

A ncient trees have long had a special place in the affections of the British. Gentle green pastures shaded by massive oaks, limes and ashes are a feature of our countryside. Some of our oldest trees have been named and venerated for centuries.

The Tortworth Chestnut in Gloucestershire is an enormous and extraordinary tree. Over 800 years old, it may have begun life in a medieval orchard. The hollow, shattered trunk, bright green with algae, is impossibly gnarled and contorted – yet it still bristles with young shoots. Its massive branches surround it, long ago rooted and now tall trees themselves.

Trees over 250 years old are commonplace in our hedgerows and parks. But we have begun to take them for granted. The aging process is no longer well understood. Beyond middle age the crown of a tree reduces in size and some branches begin to die back. This is often mistaken for a sign that the whole tree is dying. Many "stag-headed" trees with a further life expectancy of two

Left: Many species of plant, animal and insect depend on dead wood for their survival. The modern habit of tidying up the countryside deprives wildlife of essential food and shelter.

hundred years or more have been tragically and unnecessarily felled. Dead wood, too, is essential to the survival of many woodland creatures. The modern habit of tidying up the countryside has caused the widespread loss of this vital habitat.

A rough estimate of a tree's age can be made by measuring the girth of the trunk about five feet from the ground and counting one inch for every year of life. Tree Preservation Orders can be issued by local authorities on request to preserve trees for public enjoyment, making it illegal to cut or damage them. However woods subject to TPOs can still be ploughed up as long as the protected trees are left standing. This is indicative of the low value placed on our woodland heritage today. A great deal of money is made from land speculation. Landowners now expect to be compensated for loss of potential profit if prevented from development. Unhappily much of our natural heritage is assessed purely in terms of immediate financial gain.

Above: A massive hollow oak around 350 years old in a Gloucestershire deer park. This old tree was already well-established when King Charles I was beheaded outside Whitehall in 1649.

*O*ur national parkland tradition derives from the Norman obsession with deer husbandry. Thirty-five deer parks were recorded in 1086 in Domesday Book. Two hundred and fifty years later there were well over 3,000. By the end of the seventeenth century the fashion had turned from livestock to landscaping. Estate owners competed with one another to create the perfect vista. Exotic trees were in great demand as status symbols and there was fierce rivalry for new imports. The sweet-chestnut and the walnut were probably introduced to Britain from Southern Europe by the Romans. The sweet chestnut now grows wild and was thought to be a native until the recent development of pollen analysis. The walnut is still an ornamental tree, as is the horse chestnut which

was introduced from Albania in the 16th century. The sycamore, a native of Central Europe, was probably introduced at about the same time to provide fast-growing shelter for moorland farmhouses and livestock. It has since become an invasive nuisance all over Britain.

A more recent scourge of our native woods is the rhododendron. Like the sycamore it is tolerant of shade and difficult to kill. Rhododendrons quickly invade native woodland, spreading beneath the trees to the eventual exclusion of all else. Imported from the Himalayas by the Victorians, rhododendrons were planted to brighten up estates throughout the country. They have naturalised and spread into woods and on to moors and heaths far outside estate boundaries.

Westonbirt Arboretum
contains some of the
first exotics of their
kind to enter Britain. If it
hadn't been for loud
public disapproval, the
entire collection would
have been ploughed
up for crops in the
1950s.

Rhododendrons are now a serious menace to
conservation. Nothing will grow in their dense
evergreen shade.

Westonbirt Arboretum in Gloucestershire, one
of the most prominent tree collections in Europe,
grew out of a nineteenth century millionaire's
passion for exotics. Some of the trees here, like the
giant redwoods flanking the old carriageway, were
the first of their kind to enter Britain. Westonbirt
is renowned for its Japanese maples. In autumn
they are stunning in their extravagance of colour.
In the 1950s the arboretum fell into neglect and
plans were made to return the land to agriculture.
Fortunately public objection to the scheme was
vocal enough to prevent the unwarranted
destruction of this valuable collection.

Beautiful now, this view of Brecon Beacons will soon be lost to the traveller behind a dense screen of evergreen conifers – unless we force forestry organisations to consider public amenity as well as profit in their future plans.

The current vogue for treating woodland as a disposable and commercial commodity has its roots in Victorian England. The building of the railways in the nineteenth century brought cheap coal to the countryside. As a result, trees became valued more for timber than as a source of energy. Native species are slow-growing compared to foreign conifers like spruce and larch and it became fashionable to plant these exotics instead. Since conifers are killed when felled and must be replanted, woodland was less often seen as a self-sustaining resource and our native woods fell into neglect. By 1950 it was rare for a wood to be coppiced and associated trades, like furniture and tool-making and the weaving of hurdles and baskets, disappeared from the countryside. In the last 60 years we have lost half of our ancient woods.

Left: A few solitary trees are all that remains of the oakwoods which once covered these hills in mid Wales. Monotonous spruce plantations completely swamp surrounding hills.

Below: Deciduous larch offers bright relief in modern conifer plantations. Since the larch loses its needles in winter, a wider range of wildlife is able to survive in its shade.

Our demand for wood pulp, used to manufacture paper, has grown at a phenomenal rate. In the days of the Empire we satisfied this demand by importing other nations' timber. The First World War made this more difficult. In 1919 the Forestry Commission was set up to encourage the expansion of plantation forestry at home. From 1945 onwards, foresters began to concentrate on replanting native woodland with conifers. More of our ancient woods were destroyed between 1950 and 1978 than in the preceding four hundred years. We are only now beginning to dismantle the system of privileges and public subsidy which has supported the uncontrolled expansion of plantation forestry. Conservation groups have forced the government to value ancient woodland in its own right. Many woods have recently seen a return to coppicing.

More of
Britain's ancient
woods were
destroyed
between 1950
and 1978 than
in the preceding
400 years.

Modern plantations of Norway and Sitka spruce cover the landscape with an oppressive and unchanging dark green blanket. Trees are planted as close together as possible in straight rows to make maximum use of the land, to encourage the growth of straight trunks, to facilitate the use of heavy machinery and reduce labour costs. The resulting forests are hostile to most of our wildlife. Sunlight seldom reaches the forest floor. There is no undergrowth of brambles, saplings, flowers and grasses and none of the associated insects, mammals and birds. These silent forests are our modern replacement for the species-rich woodlands of the past.

Moorland throughout Britain is being prepared for conifers at an extraordinary rate. The land is scarred by thousands of drainage channels, spaced about one yard apart, extending in parallel lines from the roadside to the distant horizon. Before young conifers are planted on the ridges of soil between the channels, the ground is treated with herbicides, fungicides and pesticides to kill off the natural vegetation and reduce the risk of disease. Drainage lowers the water table. Bogs, streams and lochs dry up. Erosion becomes a problem as the binding vegetation is destroyed. Rain washes the soil away and spreads a lethal chemical cocktail over surrounding land, destroying the natural conditions of life.

The lure of public subsidy and tax benefits have encouraged private organisations, like Fountain Forestry, to plant millions of conifers, especially in Scotland. Millions more are planned. But even if we devote all of our remaining undeveloped land to modern forestry, we will make little impression on our dependence on imported timber. There is no good reason for the further destruction of rare and irreplaceable historic landscapes – ancient coppices, watermeadows, heaths, marshes and blanket bogs – in order to plant even more conifers. Neither can we justify any increase in afforestation of our national parks and other areas of outstanding natural beauty. A widespread return to traditional woodland management of native trees would create a healthier environment for wildlife. Although slower-growing than spruce and larch, the Scots pine produces top grade timber and is resistant to local pests. Why seek to

Woodland as a disposable commodity: inside a plantation of Norway spruce. Only 20 feet from the boundary and the forest floor is virtually devoid of life. Planted on blanket bog in the Flow Country of northern Scotland, this plantation has replaced a landscape of international scientific importance.

alter the land when we can encourage what grows well here?

We are all partly responsible for this unhappy change. The choices we make as consumers about the amount of packaging we need, the quantity of newspapers and magazines we buy, the timber we use, the junk mail we receive, recycling waste paper – all such choices have a far-reaching effect on the landscape. If we really want to preserve our woodland heritage, then we must consider what we buy. Look for recycled goods – pressure groups and consumer preference have forced manufacturers to take the environment into account. Most of the conifers planted go to satisfy our constant demand for paper. We should use less and recycle more. The new "green" lobby has made it fashionable rather than quirky to care about conservation. Advertisers are jumping on the bandwagon. Cynical or not, the result is good for the environment.

The next time you use the lawn mower, take note, you are about to perform an ecological experiment. You don't believe me? Well, stop mowing the lawn for a few years and watch what happens. Slowly but surely your precious greensward will be swallowed up by bushes, some of which will turn into trees. By mowing the lawn you are expending energy, either your own or energy from fossil fuels, to hold back the natural processes of succession. Whether you know it or not, you are kept busy each year maintaining an anthropogenic sub-climax called grassland. You could also do it with the aid of a match, when the end result would be heathland – especially if your garden were situated on sand.

It's not just gardeners either. Just think of all those "please keep off the grass" notices and the miles of roadside verge which are kept short cut by crews of gang mowers roaring up and down. Yes, there are places like blind corners on our roads and in formal parts of parks where greensward with a short back and sides is of great importance. But regularly mowing the rest of it is just a waste of time, energy and conservation opportunity.

It would be great if our roadside verges from motorways to country lanes could be managed as they were in the past by lengthmen – a sort of gamekeeper cum groundsperson in charge of a certain stretch of what should, in reality, be linear nature reserves. It should be their task to keep the drains open, the hedges well-laid, and the grass mown when necessary for the safety of both motorists and of local wildlife.

Already we are seeing money being spent on badger tunnels, toad crossings and vergeside reserves. The real challenge is maintaining all the rest. We should aim to create a diverse green network, linking

Keeping the trees *off* the grass

together the new set aside landscape and bringing nature reserves right into our own back yards – all one million acres of them. There could be multi millions of mini-meadows at the bottom of our gardens.

Everybody with a garden should have three different patches of grass. They needn't be very big, a few square feet will do. Each patch should be allowed to grow to a different height, being cut or mown at different times of the year. Real estate management stuff. Your eighth of an acre suddenly takes on new dimensions with great capabilities. The short meadow should be mown regularly with the blades never set below one and a half inches. The medium height area should be left until early July each year and then regularly cut. The tall patch should be left until early September and not cut until all the late summer flowers have set their seed. This is very important because you are aiming to create a self-propagating area, an area of lasting beauty. Always remove the clippings to the compost heap, for, within reason, the poorer the soil becomes, the better for wildlife.

Just think of it, an annual crop of sorrels, knapweeds, scabious, dog daisies and corn-flowers all growing nice and tall at the back. Then cats ears, cowslips, hawkweeds, harebells, lady's bedstraw, lesser stitchwort, sheepsbit, yarrow and yellow rattle growing less tall in the mid-ground. With daisies, eyebright, lambs lettuce, selfheal, speedwell and even moonwort growing as little ones in the short grass at the front. Our common countryside plants becoming commonplace once again – all thanks to you. With local suppliers like the B.T.C.V. and the R.S.N.C. beginning to provide local genetic stock, the future is certainly looking more colourful for our butterflies.DB

Monuments of ancient
civilisations have
become important
sanctuaries for the
grasslands their people
created. Steep
downland escarpments
have been spared the
plough. On army
ranges our pastoral
heritage survives at the
expense of public
access. Many ancient
monuments succumb
to the tank.

Right and Below:
Pewsey Downs
Opposite: Westbury
White Horse

Many of our traditional grassland plants
were once common on the open tundra
which covered Britain after the last ice
age. As trees gradually colonised the land, typical
grassland flowers like oxeye daisies, rock-roses and
meadow saxifrage became much less widespread.
By analysing the remains of plants buried thousand
of years ago in Britain's peat bogs, we have found
that grassland species suddenly became more
abundant about 4,000 years ago when mankind
began to clear the ancient wildwood.

Our open downlands are the legacy of
prehistoric farmers who cleared the hills of trees for

their livestock. Continuous grazing kept the trees at bay and encouraged the re-establishment of grassland. Places like the South Downs, the Yorkshire Wolds and the Chilterns are full of reminders of our ancient past. Neolithic henges and Bronze Age burial mounds are scattered over the plains and Iron Age forts are found on prominent hilltops. White horses and figures, cut into the steep flanks of chalk hills, are well-preserved on downland in Wiltshire, Dorset and Berkshire.

Monuments of ancient civilisations have become valuable sanctuaries for the grasslands their people created. Most of these public places have escaped the ravages of modern farming. The grass in summer is still golden and bright with flowers, not vivid green and poor in variety like so much of that which is fed with chemical fertilisers and herbicides. Plant communities here are the living heritage of many centuries of pastoral farming.

The use of downland for military training has saved ancient grassland from the plough but only at the expense of public access. Heavy tanks and regular shelling are destroying a wealth of archaeological treasures.

Below bottom: Bloody crane's-bill *(Geranium sanguineum)*
Below: Sainfoin *(Onobrychis viciifolia)*
Left: Pyramidal orchid *(Anacamptis pyramidalis)*
Right: Common toadflax *(Linaria vulgaris)*

Above: Centuries of grazing have left parallel tracks across our oldest downland. Grazing tracks on Pewsey Downs flow like waves down to the arable plain. Continued light grazing prevents the invasion of trees and shrubs while allowing plants to flower.

Nomads, pastoralists, burners and grazers were the makers of Britain's grasslands and plantlife had to adapt to their regime. Centuries of light grazing have produced extraordinary species-rich pastures. Spring cowslips and summer vetches, bright yellow rock-roses and delicate orchids bloom each year amongst a host of other flowering plants. Tiny fragments of this old grassland survive on steep slopes and in tight corners that have proved too awkward for modern farm machinery to plough. Here the seasons are still characterised by the predominant colours of their flowers – yellow in spring; blue, pink and white in summer; purple and mauve in autumn.

A square yard of old pasture on chalk downland can contain as many as 40 different plant species. They are able to co-exist in such density because each species has adapted to exploit the environment in a different way. Growing conditions are tough. Soils are poor and the exposed hills are at the mercy of the weather.

Downland plantlife has adapted to the shepherd's regime. Poor in soil and rich in variety, up to 40 species may grow on one square yard of pasture. Flowering strips of unploughed grassland are a vital refuge for Britain's butterflies.

Under pressure from grazing, parched in summer and frozen in winter, each plant must compete for water, minerals and light. These constraints prevent plants from reaching their full potential and a delicate balance is achieved in which no one species can dominate.

The rich mixture of plants on remaining fragments of ancient grassland will only survive if grazing continues. Their summer flowers are vital to butterflies – the common blue , the adonis and chalk-hill blue, skippers, ringlets, marbled whites, fritillaries and many others – so grazing must be light enough to allow plants to bloom. The old notion that there should always be a mouthful left when the stock are taken out is a good recipe for wildlife conservation. Species-rich pastures can be recreated from seed, but it may take up to 150 years before the delicate balance of nutrients, exposure and grazing pressure is again achieved which allows so many different plants to coexist. Low levels of nitrates and phosphates are essential if aggressive species are not to dominate.

Above: Ploughing up a burial mound on Dorset downland.

Right: Salisbury Plain: less than 100 years ago, these rolling hills were open public places, grazed by sheep and cattle. Now intensive arable farming is causing serious soil erosion. Ploughing fields down the slope greatly adds to the problem.

During the Second World War much of Britain's ancient pasture was ploughed up for cereal production in a national drive towards self-sufficiency. After the War, this policy was not abandoned. Instead, farmers were encouraged by the government to adopt increasingly intensive methods of food production. This has largely been achieved by subsidising the use of chemical fertilisers, particularly nitrates. An enormous amount of public money has been poured into the intensification of agriculture. "Improvement" grants have encouraged farmers to give up traditional farming and change the face of the British countryside. Organic farmers have had to forego financial assistance and face almost overwhelming and unfair competition from heavily subsidised intensive farms.

Farmers have been paid to plough up ancient pastures, meadows, commons, footpaths and bridleways, to uproot woods and hedgerows and fill in ponds and ditches in order to create vast prairies devoted to cereal production. Improvement has become synonymous with the ever-increasing subsidy and application of artificial fertilisers, herbicides, fungicides and insecticides. In 1963 farmers used about 500,000 tonnes of nitrogen in fertilisers. In 1984 that figure had risen to nearly 1,600,000 tonnes. As major beneficiaries of this programme of public funding, chemical companies have spent millions of pounds persuading farmers and governments to use their products. Little has been done to stop this dependence on the chemical industry, despite enormous improvements in crop yields, huge surpluses of grain and unacceptably high levels of nitrates in our water supply.

Where grazing continues, farmers have been encouraged to keep far more animals on the land than ever before. They have been paid to plough up natural grassland and reseed it with commercial grasses, typically a monoculture of rye grass, or to treat existing grassland with herbicides and chemical fertilisers – either way its floral legacy is destroyed. A single application of fertiliser can have a disastrous and long-lasting effect on the complex ecology of our oldest grasslands. Delicate species like clustered bellflowers and orchids are quickly eliminated by more aggressive competitors. Once the soil has been ploughed, many flowers seem never to return. Gentians, pasque flowers and pinks will only grow on soils that have been undisturbed for centuries. Over eighty per cent of our chalk and limestone grasslands have now been lost or irrevocably damaged.

Pale grey pavements in a limestone landscape, laid bare by glaciers and carved by the rain into gullies and crevasses.

Left: In the absence of intensive grazing, dense mats of wild thyme bloom in the summer grass.

Below: Over-grazing by sheep and concentrated public access are locally causing serious soil erosion on Britain's limestone grasslands.

*T*he close-cropped sheep pastures of the Yorkshire Dales in the north of England are still fragrant with wild thyme and full of lark song in summer, although over-grazing and millions of walkers are locally causing serious problems of erosion, especially along the Pennine Way. This pleasant landscape of traditional grassland and drystone walls contains some remarkable geological relicts. Large level expanses of pale grey rock are exposed on some of the hills. Stripped of soil and vegetation by the passage of glaciers, these "limestone pavements" are a reminder of Britain after the last ice age.

Limestone pavements were once sheets of solid rock, scoured smooth by the action of the ice and its burden of debris. Thousands of years later, water has dissolved and removed the limestone along cracks and joints, cutting a pattern of fissures into the rock and dividing it into individual, irregularly shaped "paving stones" known as clints, separated by narrow gullies or grikes, usually only a few inches wide and up to ten feet deep. Grazing sheep prevent plants from growing above the surface of this bizarre and convoluted natural maze.

Above: Beyond the reach of grazing sheep, a hart's-tongue fern flourishes in the moist shelter of a grike.

Right: Strange reminders of Britain after the last ice age, limestone pavements are rapidly being destroyed for rockery stone. Once destroyed, they can't be replaced.

From a distance, limestone pavements can seem barren places, hostile to life. Walking across them, however, you find a wealth of plants hidden from sight in the deeper grikes. Many flowers and ferns flourish in their moist shelter. Conditions are similar to those on the woodland floor. Rare woodland species like herb-Paris, Solomon's seal and lilies-of-the-valley can be found growing alongside plants of more rocky habitats. On sheep-grazed pavements, the stunted forms of trees and shrubs remain confined within these natural rock gardens. Without grazing, woodland develops. Yews and junipers sometimes form extensive prostrate skirts over the surface of the stone.

Limestone pavements have long provided stone for walls, gate posts and buildings. In the past the clints were removed individually with simple tools. Today they are torn apart by tractors and explosives and even the most massive pavements are at risk. Nearly half of our limestone pavements have been badly damaged. Only three per cent remain unexploited. Some are now more like open-cast mines. Ironically, most of the stone is sold in garden centres. Many people buying rockery stone don't realise that they are causing the destruction of an extraordinary landscape of international scientific importance. Limestone pavements took thousands of years to form. Once destroyed, they cannot be replaced.

From January to April traditional pasture is not very productive and cannot support livestock. Before the mechanisation of farming, horses and oxen drawing the ploughs had their greatest burden of work during these lean months. To keep livestock well-fed throughout the winter, farmers reserved their best grassland for making hay. Very few of these ancient hay meadows have survived. Hay production is no longer a vital part of the farming year. Summer fields tall with fragrant grasses and rich in flowering plants are now rare in the British countryside. Meadow saffron once bloomed in abundance after the hay was harvested. Now the delicate pink flowers are mostly confined to a few fields dotted over the south of England.

Britain's richest meadows are on the floodplains of rivers. Some have been irrigated since the 16th century. Water led off from weirs was distributed over the fields through an elaborate system of channels, then returned to the river further downstream. Nutrients in the riverwater enriched the soils, giving rise to exceptionally productive grassland. The "drowners" who maintained these water-meadows were accomplished professionals, well-respected for their skills. Most of the evidence of their work has been destroyed since the 1940s. Irrigation channels have been ploughed up and luxuriant meadows drained. The little that remains deserves to be protected for its historical and botanical significance.

Left: Cowslips have rapidly disappeared from the countryside as meadows and pastures have been ploughed and reseeded.

Right: Meadow Saffron was once a common sight on autumn meadows after hay-making.

North Meadow at Cricklade is an important reminder of all we have lost. The common grazing rights of local people here have protected the land from agricultural "improvement". The grass is allowed to grow in summer and from April until July the meadow is a mass of flowers. A part of the meadow is harvested for seed each year, helping us to recreate similar grassland throughout the country. Among the first of the plants to bloom is the snake's-head fritillary. Once common in meadows throughout the Thames valley, the many thousands which still bloom each spring at Cricklade are nearly all that is left of this species in the wild in Britain.

100 years ago, snake's-head fritillaries were common throughout the Thames valley. Now almost the entire British population is confined to a single Wiltshire meadow. A legal anomaly has left common grazing rights intact, saving this unusual flower from virtual extinction in the wild.

Poppies in a field of wheat in Somerset: many farmland weeds are now so uncommon that they must be treated as rare wild flowers. Left unplanted and unsprayed, awkward bits of fields can become valuable nature reserves.

Below: Mayweed and poppies

Below Bottom: Field pansies *(Viola arvensis)*

Some of Britain's farmland weeds were found on naturally disturbed land like sand dunes and river terraces before the advent of cultivation. Others, like poppies and plantains, were imported inadvertently in the grain of early settlers and had their origins in southern Europe, the Mediterranean and Asia. The Romans introduced many plants for medicinal and culinary use. Ground-elder, now a troublesome and common garden weed, was originally imported as a salad vegetable. Ragwort, another invasive weed, can be very destructive of grassland if left unchecked.

Efficient methods of sorting seed, crop-breeding, stubble-burning, the use of herbicides and more intensive farming have all but eliminated many of our agricultural weeds. Marginal land has been ploughed and inorganic fertilisers have made it possible to sow a new crop soon after harvest.

The reservoir of seeds in the soil, particularly of cornfield weeds, is constantly being depleted. Plants that were once an expensive nuisance are now a rare delight. Poppies and corncockles, wild pansies and corn marigolds cling to life at the margins of huge fields of grain.

Many farmland weeds have become so uncommon that they must now be treated as rare wild flowers. Pheasant's-eye, wild candytuft, red star-thistle, cornflowers. . . the list of endangered species is long. Other more common species are declining rapidly.

With sympathetic treatment field margins can become important nature reserves. Protected from fertilisers and pesticides, and ploughed every one or two years, they provide food for insects, shelter for small animals and farmland birds like the partridge, as well as adding a welcome splash of colour to the rural landscape.

Left: Red campion at a Cornish roadside.
Above: Yellow loosestrife in the Peak District.

Right: Tufted vetch, lady's bedstraw, red campion and buttercups on a lane in Yorkshire.

Drystone walls throughout Britain are sadly falling into disrepair. There has recently been a welcome resurgence of interest in the skills of traditional roadside management.

Carefully controlled roadside maintenance is rewarded with colourful displays of wild flowers.

Roadsides that have escaped modern herbicides and our obsession with tidiness have become important sanctuaries for wildlife. Hedgerows full of the scent of honeysuckle are sometimes all that remains of ancient woods. Hedges often contain grassland plants like sweet briar and dog roses that have vanished from surrounding fields.

Traditional skills of roadside management are also disappearing from the countryside. Hedges are no longer cut and laid to form an effective barrier to livestock. Indiscriminately hacked about with mechanical trimmers, oblivious to nesting birds, budding flowers, saplings and seeding plants, hedges have become a ragged shambles and are often grubbed up to be replaced with wire fencing, both at tax payers expense. Drystone walls, covered in plants of rocky habitats like stone-crop and navelwort, are also falling into neglect.

Many lanes in Hampshire, Essex and Dorset are certainly 1,000 years old. Some are more ancient still. Long-established colonies of stitchwort and campion, orchids and harebells bloom in profusion at the roadside. Many beautiful lanes in Cornwall and Devon follow prehistoric field patterns and are probably of the same age. Their ancient walls, banked up with soil over the centuries, are a mass of primroses, violets and bluebells in spring, and orchids and foxgloves in summer. Banks and verges need to be cut or mown in autumn and early spring to retain their full complement of species.

In counties where roadside management has been carefully controlled, the reward has been a procession of flowers throughout the year. Nonetheless, over 130,000 miles of hedgerow have been ripped up since the War. Taxpayers have spent millions to subsidise their removal. Between 1980 and 1985 hedges were destroyed at a rate of about 4,000 miles a year.

Dorset Heath (*Erica ciliaris*) is becoming increasingly rare as its habitat is destroyed. Always of marginal farming importance, our heaths should never have been put to the plough. It was a total waste of time, effort and tax payers' money.

The popular idea of heaths as barren wastelands belies a long history of exploitation. Heathland, like so much of the British countryside, is a product of human activity — the result of woodland clearance and grazing on land with poor, sandy soils. The fundamental plants of heathland — heather, gorse and bracken — are rejuvenated in a similar way to trees if cut or burnt. Heather was used for thatching and is an important source of nectar for honeybees. Gorse was an important domestic fuel, making a hot and fragrant fire. Bracken, now generally despised for its invasive nature, was once a useful product of heathland management. In the 18th and 19th century burning bracken provided the potash used in glass, soap and detergent production. It was also fuel for brick-furnaces and litter for livestock.

Rabbits were introduced to Britain in the Middle Ages and warrens for their commercial production were set up on heaths throughout the country. Some were still in operation sixty years ago. Rabbit meat and fur have since become unfashionable and farming has almost stopped, but this ancient heathland practice is still recalled in place names like Lakenheath Warren. Grazing rabbits were an important part of heathland ecology. The rabbit population was decimated by the deliberate introduction of the appalling disease myxomatosis. In the absence of any other grazing or management, many of our heaths reverted to woodland.

Heathland is very restricted in its worldwide distribution. Extensive areas once found along the northwest coast of Europe have largely been destroyed. Heathland was once extensive in

Cornwall, Dorset, Hampshire, Suffolk, Surrey and
Sussex. Although much has been lost in the past
fifty years, Britain's heaths are still some of the
best remaining examples in Europe. Some
regionally-occurring heathers like Dorset heath
and Cornish heath and beautiful plants of wet
heath, like the marsh gentian, are now becoming
quite rare. Habitat loss is a growing threat to the
survival of species indigenous to heathland like
ladybird spiders, smooth snakes and sand lizards.
Scarce birds like the nightjar use its scrubby
shelter, whilst birds of prey like the hobby need its
wide open spaces.

Looking across
Middlebere Heath
towards Corfe Castle.

*T*he Dorset heathlands, made famous in the prose of Thomas Hardy, can be sombre places in winter. But in spring, gorse and bog myrtle start to bloom and their flowers fill the air with the scent of coconut and bitter almonds. Summer spreads a fragrant carpet of purple heather over the ground. Its colour lasts until early autumn. Dorset heathlands are amongst the very few places in Britain where all six of our native reptiles still occur together – the viviparous lizard and the sand lizard, the slow worm, the smooth snake and grass snake and the adder. They are a last refuge for the sand lizard and the heath grasshopper, and their gorse bushes provide food and shelter for the rare Dartford warbler.

Dorset's heathland runs down to the sea at Studland Bay. Open expanses of heather, broken by marshy pools and patches of woodland, give way to brilliant white sand dunes. The parched ground is encrusted with lichens and mosses. Approaching the shore, heather grows alongside marram grass until at last it is defeated by the mobile sands at the water's edge. The beach here is beautiful and a favourite haunt of naked bathers. Although access is restricted, the enormous number of people who come here in summer is a serious threat to the ecology of the region. Fires started in the dry scrub spread quickly and are a constant danger to the environment.

A blanket of heather on the white sand dunes of Studland Bay. Britain's heaths are some of the best examples of their kind in Europe. Our lowland heaths are now so fragmented that fire is a constant threat to their survival.

British
taxpayers have
paid to be
excluded from
more of the
countryside than
ever before.

*H*uge expanses of Dorset heathland have
been lost to agriculture and commercial
forestry in the last 150 years. The Ministry
of Defence owns a large part of the heath today and
they too have planted thousands of conifers.
Europe's largest onshore oilfield is here, with all
its pipelines, access roads and power supplies.
Mineral extraction also takes its toll on the land –
ball clay for the potteries, sand and gravel for the
construction industry. Gravel is used extensively
in the building of roads; our massive new
programme of road building will mean even more
ugly pits will be excavated from the heathland.
There are also plans to build a nuclear powerstation
in the centre of the heath.

At the beginning of the nineteenth century,
Bournemouth was a small coastal village. Now it
is the home of almost half a million people and a
booming tourist centre. One of Europe's fastest
growing towns, Bournemouth sits in the heart of a
dwindling habitat of international importance.
Pressure for further urban development is intense.
Meanwhile, rhododendrons, pines and birches are
invading remaining undeveloped heath, and
uncontrolled motorcycle scrambling and horse-
riding is causing severe erosion problems.

Since the 1930s Dorset heathland has been
destroyed at a rate of about 750 acres per year. The
rate of loss has slowed since the seventies but it has
by no means stopped. The area has now been
declared a Site of Special Scientific Interest.

Twenty-seven per cent of the heath is owned and
cared for by conservation bodies, but most of the
rest is in private hands and its future is precarious.
The number of species present on heathland is
directly related to the size of the heath. Dorset's
heathlands are becoming increasingly fragmented.
Many species are on the verge of extinction. This
precious habitat is struggling for survival against
most of the major demands of modern society.
Whether it survives is up to us.

Sand and gravel pits in
the heart of Dorset's
heathland. We have
destroyed three
quarters of our
internationally
important heathland in
the last 50 years.

I spent the formative years of my life in Carshalton and Cheam in Surrey. The whole area at the foot of the chalk downs was then a watery wonderland. Bubbling springs fed the village ponds and a Bourne river rose every seven (or was it four) years to fill the numerous ditches and pools in Nonesuch Park, just as they had since the time of Henry 8th. We could even dig our garden in Brickfields Lane and clear water would soon fill each and every excavation.

The draw down of urbanisation changed all that. Now the waters are once more beginning to flow as industry declines in the London basin. But the once-pure springs are now tainted with nitrate leaching from ploughed downland swards. Nevertheless, the memories are still there and it is to them that I owe a lifetime of total fascination,

immersed both physically and academically in water and its most down to earth product, peat.

Our rivers and lakes became grotesquely polluted and our farmponds were annihilated not, I believe, with malice aforethought, but out of expediency. Progress swept everything before it, producing jobs, consumer goods and the desires and devices of labour saving economies. Our environment suffered, nothing more so than our atmosphere and our water. The former was greatly improved by the Clean Air Act of 1956. The latter has taken much longer, mainly because it was less obvious to the general public and simple sand filtration kept our home supplies pure and potable.

The call for clean up came about as a by-product of the leisure industry. As more and more sports fishermen took to Britain's rivers, they lent their

Peat, *glorious* peat

increasing weight (unfortunately some of it was loaded with lead) to the clean up argument. Since the last World War, three new distinctive forces have built up on this particular horizon; the canalisation and taming of our streams and rivers and the draining of our self-purifying water meadows; the development of factory farms for cereals, livestock and even fish; and the demise of the compost heap, its products replaced since the sixties with peat dug mainly from our lowland fens and bogs.

Times are fortunately changing fast. The demise of the old water-guzzling sunset industries is resulting in the rise of water tables. Ponds are being re-excavated and refilled with water in farms, schools and urban gardens. Old gravel pits are being left to fill with water, wildlife and windsports. The fishing fraternity are phasing out lead weights. (If only the

shooting fraternity could phase out lead shot. A ceramic shot which eventually broke down to release lime would solve a lot of problems.) Factory farming and high input-high output farming is coming under the control of environmental legislation and economic constraints.

When it comes to ground water enrichment, it must, however, be emphasised that organic husbandry doesn't have all the answers – although it certainly is an improvement on the current state of affairs. The demise of our peatlands has at last been addressed by a public appeal from the R.S.N.C., the R.S.P.B., F.O.E., B.A.N.C. and Plantlife. Public response has been amazing. We must now get our acts still further together and get the heaps composting once more and the alternatives dug into garden centres. Our rivers, streams, lakes and wetlands must live again. DB

Persuading people that peat bogs are beautiful is not easy. They have an unfortunate reputation as dreary, treacherous places, eager to suck the unwary down to an evil-smelling end. In fact they are not particularly dangerous – the most you usually risk is a boot full of water. Neither are they unhealthy places. Peat bog is a particularly sterile environment – so much so that the mosses which grow on its surface were used to dress wounds during the First World War.

Surviving fragments of the prehistoric landscape, some peat bogs have been growing for over 7,000 years. Peat bog forms on land that is constantly waterlogged. Dead vegetation is prevented from rotting by a lack of oxygen and over the centuries it accumulates as a thick layer of peat. Most of the available nutrients are bound into this virtually impermeable layer so that any plants growing on it must depend on the chemicals dissolved in rainwater for growth. Few ordinary plants are able to grow here. Those that do, have developed some remarkable methods of survival.

Peat bog on the shores of Loch Maree – a patchwork of reedy pools, tangled heather and sage-green mossy hummocks.

A colourful mosaic of exotic plantlife lies at your feet on Britain's peat bogs. Sphagnum mosses, ranging from lime-green to burgundy-red, form extensive carpets over the ground. These mosses hold rainwater like a sponge, creating their own reservoir of nutrients and providing a source of water in times of drought. Some plants have even evolved to trap and digest insects: scarlet sundews and butterworts with delicate violet-like flowers, ensnare flies on sticky filaments. Bladderworts in watery hollows set ingenious under-water traps for small aquatic creatures. Their yellow flowers, like miniature sweetpeas, colour the summer boglands.

Many objects buried in peat bogs thousands of years ago remain perfectly preserved there today. By studying the contents of bogs we have learnt a great deal about the development of Britain's climate and vegetation. Animals and even human bodies have been discovered. The trunks of trees buried long ago have been dug up for fuel for centuries. The peat itself has been cut and dried for fuel throughout the history of human settlement and it continues to provide warmth and power for many people today. The compost and "grow pots" which fill our garden centres are made from peat deriving from these bogs. In fact moss peat has been the mainstay of the modern horticultural industry.

Above: Oblong-leaved sundew. Tall, leafless stems topped with small white flowers spring from the centre of the plant in summer. Insects become trapped on sticky filaments on the leaves and are slowly digested by the plant.

Top: The living skin of Britain's bogs, brightly coloured sphagnum mosses hold rainwater like a sponge. Specialised bog plants depend on the nutrients dissolved in rainwater for growth.

Right: Bog asphodel
with bright yellow
summer flowers. Its
autumn leaves and
fruits colour the
boglands a rich burnt
orange.

Bogs were found on farmland throughout Britain, before it became fashionable to drain all marginal land. Wet hollows, white with downy cotton grass, and rough pasture full of the canary-yellow flowers of bog-asphodel were once a common feature of the countryside. Large areas of Somerset, Lancashire and East Anglia were covered in extensive blankets of peat. Where fragments still remain, the living skin of Sphagnum moss has usually been destroyed. Blanket bogs are still extensive in parts of Wales and Scotland and in the Pennines. Their many pools are important refuges for the aquatic stages in the lifecycle of dragonflies.

Blanket bog, many feet thick in places, extends for 150 miles over the hills and plains of northern Scotland. Until very recently these boglands, known as the Flow Country, had survived intact in spite of thousands of years of human exploitation. Agricultural reclamation, moor-burning and commercial peat-winning had accounted for some losses but their effect here was less devastating than it was further south. But now huge tracts of bog have been drained and planted with conifers. One of the natural wonders of Europe is slowly dying.

Conifer plantations do not do well on blanket bog without the copious addition of fertilisers. Rain washes these chemical additives over the surrounding land, upsetting the delicate balance of nutrients on its growing surface. Bogland plants are particularly sensitive to drainage since they depend on a reservoir of rainwater for growth. Starved of water and with an over-dose of nutrients, the living sphagnum layer is eventually destroyed. Erosion becomes a problem as the bog dries out.

Reedy pools disappear from the landscape and thousands of years of history are carried away on the wind.

Very few, if any, of Britain's bogs have escaped impoverishment at the hands of modern forestry and farming. Ranked at the bottom of the league of popular beauty spots, they are unlikely to survive intact without immediate action from those who care.

Right: A watery hollow
on a moorland farm,
still undrained and
graced with downy
cotton grass.
Dragonflies depend on
unpolluted shallow
pools for their survival.

Far Right: Rannoch
Moor – a great expanse
of golden deer grass,
boggy pools and reed-
filled lochans.
Uncontrolled burning
of blanket bog for
grouse, sheep and
deer grazing causes
long-term damage to
wildlife and severe
erosion in times of
drought.

Right: Marsh helleborine – an orchid of our grazing marshes, once widespread but now becoming increasingly rare largely as a result of fenland drainage.

Below: Grass of Parnassus – typical of fens with a high calcium content in the water.

Over fifty years ago, fenlands and marshes were still frequent around lakes and on the floodplains of rivers. Reedswamps teeming with waterfowl and dense beds of sedges grew around stretches of open water. Rivers fringed with bulrushes meandered through lush grassland, where meadowsweet, angelica and valerian grew shoulder-high. Marsh marigolds and yellow flags flowered in damp hollows and water-lilies floated on quiet pools. Orchids were plentiful, as were dragonflies, herons, frogs, grass snakes and swallowtail butterflies.

In the past waterlands were feared and mistrusted places – the French Revolution actually abolished all marshes by statute – but they had a lot to offer. Fish and waterfowl were abundant. Reeds and sedges could be harvested and used for thatching and fuel. Peat, too, could be cut for fuel. In spite of this, a long history of human settlement has been concerned mainly with the destruction of our fenlands. Roman engineers built an artificial watercourse 90 miles long to drain the land between Lincoln and Cambridge. Anglo-Saxon and medieval farmers built huge earthen embankments to prevent flooding and created the extraordinarily rich grasslands once so characteristic of fenland.

Over the past 400 years we have spent an enormous amount of money and effort trying to convert land better suited to grazing into fields of grain. Rivers feeding the wetlands have been intercepted, diverted and straightened. Meres have

been drained and marshlands ploughed. Water has been constantly pumped out of the land, gradually lowering the water-table. Since 1945 advances in drainage technology, bulldozers and massive public subsidy have almost defeated Britain's ancient wetlands. Grazing cattle and fenland pastures have been replaced by combine harvesters and monotonous prairies devoted entirely to arable farming. Rivers and drainage channels are awash with fertilisers, and any remaining pools and reedbeds tend to be treated as convenient dumps for agricultural and household waste.

A damp hollow on the flood plain of the River Wye. Surrounded by pollarded willow and alder and fringed with reeds, such pools are a vital refuge for wildlife.

Drifts of pale milkmaids
and yellow flag irises
were once a common
sight. With 20% of
agricultural land
coming out of
production, cattle could
again graze
contentedly on flower-
filled wetland pastures.

An abandoned cart in
Mound Alder Woods.
Less than 200 years
ago this was an open
expanse of sea. Now it
is Britain's largest
wetland wood.

*I*solated fragments of fenland vegetation still
remain on land that has proved difficult to
drain. Management for nature is essential if
their full range of wildlife is to survive. Since
surrounding water levels have been drastically
lowered, it is often necessary to pump water into
reserves in summer. Finding a water supply
unaffected by fertilisers and pollutants is usually
impossible.

Continued grazing of marshland is important to
the survival of many fenland flowers like grass-of-
Parnassus, marsh helleborine and the fen orchid.
Some species depend on the regular harvesting of
reeds and sedges. Birds of the reedswamps like the
marsh harrier, the bittern, the water rail and the
reed bunting – are now very rare in Britain.
Farmponds and ditches are fast disappearing,
along with their population of toads, newts and
frogs. Four species of dragonfly have become
extinct since 1953; many others need urgent
protection.

The development of woodland on abandoned
wetland meadows creates serious problems for
their conservation, but wetland woods are also a
rarity in our countryside. An embankment was
built in 1816 across the end of Loch Fleet on the
northeast coast of Scotland, stopping the sea one
and a half miles short of the natural hightide limit.
Silt carried by rivers has gradually built up on the
landward side, creating ideal growing conditions
for reeds, sedges and trees. Mound Alder Woods
are now a lichen-covered tangle of alder, willow
and water-mint. One of Britain's largest wetland
woods has established itself here on land claimed
from the sea less than 200 years ago.

The River Shiel in spate after a week of heavy rain.

Right: A small stream runs below Craig Ddu in the mountains of Montgomery to join the River Wye at Rhayader.

The generous rain on Britain's hills makes them the source of thousands of streams and rivers. Twelve main rivers rise on Dartmoor and the River Dart alone is fed by fifty-five separate tributaries. The sight and sound of running water is hard to resist. Even the hollow trickle of an underground stream has us on our knees trying to find its source. Walkers stopping to eat lunch by a mountain stream are easily tempted to stay until sunset.

Waterfalls have always been popular. Swollen by winter rains, they can be spectacular torrents, while in the heat of summer their plunge pools are revealed, carved glass-smooth in the rock. Plants and animals of upland streams and rivers have to cope with life in fast-flowing water and a seasonal cycle of flood and drought. Mosses, lichens and liverworts cling to the rocks in mid-stream. Rarities like the tiny Tunbridge filmy fern grow on more sheltered banks. Dippers and wagtails search for water insects amongst boulders green with a slimy film of algae. This is food for thousands of invertebrates, who in turn are food for trout and grayling. Fish spawn on clear gravelly stretches and oystercatchers and sandpipers nest on exposed shingle banks.

Many streams on Dartmoor were channelled into artificial watercourses to increase their gradient and provide more power for mills and forges in the valleys.

Below: Even fast flowing rivers can be silenced by the winter weather – Varragill River, Skye.

B ritain's upland streams are closely associated with human industry. We have long taken advantage of their fast-flowing currents to sift heavy metal ores from gravel and sand. Often straightened and diverted to increase their flow, streams have powered thousands of watermills, working forges and spinning textiles. Many peaceful river valleys around Britain's moors were once thriving industrial centres. Dartmoor is crossed by a network of artificial watercourses known as "leats". Some were dug over 700 years ago to turn the wheels of medieval tin mills, crushing and smelting the metal ore. Others still

provide drinking water today.

Modern hydro-electric schemes are also designed to harness the power of our upland streams and rivers. The flow is often controlled by creating a reservoir in a river's head waters. The discharge of water through the dam is regulated and can fluctuate dramatically. The seasonal cycle of flood and drought is disrupted by irregular massive surges of water and long dry spells, and the river is stripped of life for several miles below the dam. As renewable sources of power, hydro-electric schemes are a good idea, but they do have some environmental costs.

Hill drainage and afforestation can be very damaging to river life. Erosion causes irregular tides of peat and soil to flood into streams, smothering the spawning grounds of salmon and trout and muddying the clear waters. The build-up of pine needles can change the chemical balance of the water. . .and of course fertilisers, herbicides and pesticides take their toll of life here as they do almost everywhere in Britain. But in spite of these problems, this is still a country full of beautiful upland streams and rivers. Frozen solid in winter, they are an impressive symbol of the power of nature.

Below: Water forget-me-not, *Myosotis scorpioides,* common in marshes, ponds and at the edge of shallow rivers.

Right: At dawn, after a clear cold night, the River Wye shrouds its valley and distant flood plain with mist.

The flowering rush, *Butomus umbellatus,* grows by slow-moving muddy waters typical of Britain's meandering lowland rivers.

Rivers are not simply drainage channels. They create a wide range of habitats essential to many plants and animals. Lowland rivers meander through the plains between banks full of flowers. Aquatic plants anchor themselves in the muddy river bed. Herons fish in the shallows and insects breed in sluggish backwaters full of pondweed. Kingfishers and water voles make their nests in undisturbed banks, and crayfish hide amongst the submerged roots of overhanging trees.

Rivers act as corridors for the dispersal of seeds, allowing foreign introductions to spread rapidly throughout the river system. Himalayan balsam was introduced to Britain towards the end of the 19th century. It now grows in dense stands along many of our rivers and its distinctive pink flowers are a common sight in summer. The yellow and red blooms of the Monkey flower, a native of North America, are now common on Yorkshire's rivers. Another introduction, the mink has become a serious nuisance to river life, killing many birds, fish and small mammals. They are also a threat to our few remaining otters.

The structural diversity of many of Britain's rivers has been destroyed by turning them into featureless canals running straight as an arrow through the countryside. Many species have been lost due to a lack of food and breeding sites. Industrial, domestic and agricultural effluents cause many further losses. Those rivers that have escaped the ugly ravages of modern life remain places of great beauty and variety. They are an important reminder of all we once had, and a storehouse for all we could recreate, if we chose to invest in nature.

This page: The Wye is a salmon river with gravelly head waters and a tidal mouth. Along its course the river tumbles over rapids and into deep seething pools. It winds through gentle agricultural plains and spectacular wooded gorges.

Opposite: The Stour is a typical chalk river. Its surface is studded with the tiny white and yellow flowers of water crowfoot in summer. Water forget-me-nots and purple loosestrife grow tall on its banks and beds of watercress are abundant in its clear shallow waters.

Blueprints for the future.

Above: A wooded farmland brook meandering through meadowland. Kingfishers are a common sight on this stretch of Cam Brook. Fish are abundant. The banks contain a mixture of water, woodland and grassland plants.

Right: The Somerset Avon is slow-flowing. Yellow and white water-lilies grow thickly in sheltered water. Bright dragonflies and damsel flies flit above tall beds of bur-reeds and flowering rushes. Grass snakes slither from the banks and swim across the river.

Blueprints for the future.

Lakes are found on mountains and moorlands and on fertile lowland plains. They are especially abundant in Cumbria, North Wales and Scotland. Life in their waters is largely determined by altitude and the surrounding rock. Poor in phosphorous and nitrogen, two elements essential for plant growth, upland lakes can only support a limited range of wildlife. With few free-floating algae, their water is astonishingly clear. Sunlight can penetrate to considerable depths. Some mosses and plants like stonewort and quillwort are able to grow up to forty feet below the surface.

The exposed shores of our upland lakes are lined with boulders and wave-battered sandy beaches. Water lobelia and various-leaved pondweed may colonise sheltered bays, along with reeds and sedges. Fishing is excellent. Brown trout, salmon and eels are plentiful. Some Welsh lakes are home to the rare whitefish and vendace, another rare fish, seem confined to the Lake District. Many birds breed on our upland lakes – divers, teal, goosanders and the ubiquitous mallard. Loch Garten is famous for its ospreys. In spring hundreds of palmate newts breed in small lochs high in the Scottish mountains.

Lowland lakes are rich in nutrients and support a much wider range of plants and animals. The water is often pale green with a healthy growth of microscopic algae. Many types of pondweed, lilies, rushes and reeds grow in shallow water. Plants common to marsh and fenland grow around the lakeside. Countless snails, worms, shrimps and water boatmen feed amongst the rich vegetation and they are food for many species of fish like bream, chub, tench, minnows and sticklebacks. Pike also lurk in their fertile waters. Shallow lakes attract thousands of ducks in winter. At night grazing birds like geese come on to our lakes to roost.

Two hundred years of acid rain, formed mainly when sulphur dioxide and other emissions from industry and motorised vehicles dissolve in water in the atmosphere, have caused many of our lakes and rivers to become over-acidic, killing millions of fish. To save the fish, huge quantities of lime have been spread on surrounding land or dumped directly into the water. Experiments have only proved successful in the short term. Nobody knows exactly how much lime to apply. Liming around Loch Fleet in Scotland has killed ninety per cent of the bog moss in the treated area. Britain is the largest producer of sulphur-dioxide pollution in Western Europe.

Privatisation of the power industry has put a halt to research into the problem. One obvious answer is an immediate reduction in permissible levels of emissions.

Not a country lane, but the Kennet and Avon canal completely choked with red algae due to over-enrichment of the water.

Until the 1950s we thought that the lakes of Norfolk and Suffolk, known as the Broads, were entirely natural. We have since discovered that they are in fact massive flooded peat-diggings dating back to the Middle Ages and beyond. The resulting lakes have become so popular as pleasure-boating centres that they have lost much of their wildlife. Boats disturb aquatic plants and churn up the water. Bow waves erode the banks. Noise drives away breeding birds and shy animals like the otter. Tourist pressure is a growing problem in Britain's popular beauty spots.

Water pollution in the Broads has now reached catastrophic levels. Already awash with fertilisers and sewage, the added pressure of waste from thousands of summer holiday makers has caused a dramatic over-enrichment of the water. Aquatic life is choking under a dense blanket of fetid algae. Fish and waterfowl are dying. Rutland Water has suffered a similar fate. A lurid green algal bloom has covered the whole reservoir. Even sheep and pet dogs have died as a result.

Fertiliser run-off from farmland and the dumping of slurry are major causes of over-enrichment. Water authorities must carry some of the blame. They have not been obliged to control the high levels of phosphorous in sewage discharged into our rivers. The accumulated effect on Britain's lakes can be disastrous.

Problems facing the Broads are common to

Below: Unaffected by
tourist pressure, a
peaceful lake on a
private-estate on
Deeside.

Below bottom: Loch
Morlich, quiet now on a
rainy summer's
evening but suffering
under the pressure of
its many admirers.

lakes and rivers throughout the country. The
extraordinary boom in activities like wind-surfing,
aqua-biking, motor-boating, water-skiing and
sailing has turned peaceful mountain lochs into
crowded leisure centres with all their attendant
pressures and problems. Of course people should
be allowed to enjoy themselves but we must also
leave some space for wildlife – which after all gives
as many people pleasure as sport.

Many upland lakes are used as reservoirs to
provide water or electricity. Water levels fluctuate
enormously leaving a broad scar devoid of life
around the water margins. Scarring often backs for
half a mile or more up streams and rivers feeding
the reservoir.

In the last fifty
years we have
destroyed over
ninety per cent
of East Anglia's
fenland.

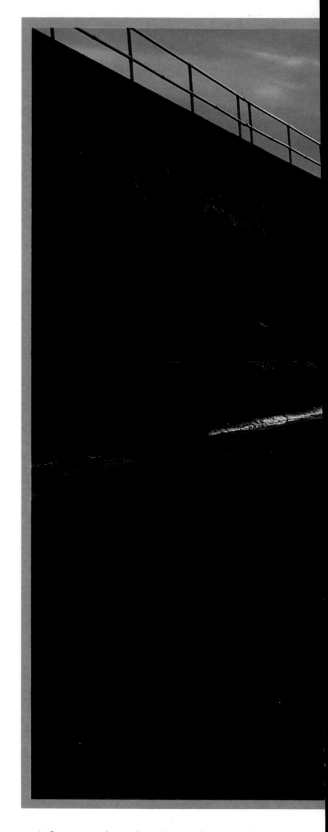

*T*he outlook for Britain's wetlands, rivers
and lakes is not entirely gloomy. Much has
survived that is still healthy and beautiful
– and it will remain this way, if we learn from our
mistakes elsewhere. With professional guidance
we can recreate much that we have lost. Many
gravel pits have been turned into lakes rich in
wildlife. Others have been reserved as water-sports
centres. Some like Pensthorpe in Norfolk have
become important sanctuaries for waterbirds. A
return to traditional management is essential in
many places. The wildlife park at Pensthorpe
includes some wonderfully lush meadowland.
There has been such a huge move away from
livestock in this county once famous for its
grasslands, that the staff find it hard even to give
the hay away.

If we are serious about protecting our
environment for the enjoyment of future
generations, then we must make sure that our
rivers and lakes are properly wardened. Discharges
into the water must be carefully monitored and the
fines imposed on polluters should be equal to the
cost of repairing the damage *and* ensuring that a
similar incident cannot happen again. Above all,
such fines must be enforceable and permissable
levels of emissions must be kept to their absolute
minimum. Some of the rivers of the densely
populated, industrial lowlands are still very badly
polluted. The cost of protecting what remains
unspoilt and cleaning up what has been destroyed
will be high. Money spent on research into
evermore intensive methods of farming could be
better spent trying to find ways to feed the world
without destroying the planet.

I really hate the idea of paving certain stretches of the Pennine Way, be it with duck boards or, perish the thought, tarmacadam. Yet if something isn't done and quickly, continuing erosion will further destroy this and other of our remote and beautiful places. Likewise in all our honeypots of tourism, people-pressure is an eroding problem. The Lake District, the Broads, fells, mountain tops, downs and dunes are all in grave danger of being loved to death. Countryscape management is a growth industry and it should not just be left to the voluntary sector, despite the fact that they do a great job.

Bodies like the C.P.R.E. campaign and counsel. The National Trust not only look after some of our great country houses but they also care for an ever-increasing area of our country estate. They own the heart of Lakeland and do their best to keep it in good fettle, complete with well-kept footpaths, slate roofs and drystone walls. These are not government-funded bodies but charities supported by ordinary people like you and me. So, too, are the Living Landscape Trust, the B.T.C.V. and Groundwork Trust. They have the expertise and, hopefully, will continue to provide the workforce to carry out vital management without which Britain's traditional countryside and much of the livelihood of the tourist industry would fall to pieces.

They are doing trojan work, and long may it continue. But I believe that we need more than that. Britain's fabulous heritage needs and deserves a Heritage Taskforce at work all the time. As

Highspots *and* honeypots

computers and robots continue to provide us all with more leisure time, opportunities must be created not only for school leavers and early retirers but also for jogging yuppies, weekending families and neighbourhood parties to opt into such schemes. The range of work to be done is not only enormous, but it can be immensely rewarding. Perhaps Prince Charles' Army will, at least in part, fill this particular bill.

Thanks to those computers and robots, I believe in the future we will only have to work for twenty hours a week for perhaps twenty years of our lives. For the rest of the time everyone should have the opportunity of doing their bit to manage our heritage, both natural and people made. In my wildest dreams I see a two year post school or university "conscription" and the revitalisation of the great Livery Companies and Guilds, with training schemes run by the Workers' Education Association and the Continuing Education Departments of our universities and technical colleges.

There is only one real problem in all of this. Not very long ago most of the people who visited Britain's wilder places appeared content to sit in their cars or play and picnic not far from the carpark, enjoying the landscape in a passive way. The more who get turned on to the countryside experience as part of the new workforce, the more boots, trainers and tyres will be focused on our remote countryside. So perhaps there will have to be corduroy tracks across some of our landscapes! The only alternative would be to ration access to our wilder places – and that would be worse than tarmac. DB

*I*n the whole of southern England only two hills rise above 2,000 feet. But on the Pennines and in Cumbria, in Wales and the Scottish Highlands many peaks reach 3,000 feet and more. Although very small compared to their counterparts on the continent, Britain's mountains still manage to look impressive. Twelve thousand years ago when the glaciers of the last ice age finally melted, they left behind a land of distinctive rounded hills, U-shaped valleys, and silent mountain lakes. Where craggy ridges remain, they dominate the landscape.

Below: The shattered quartz and sandstone peaks of Torridon. Though seemingly barren, delicate flowering plants like the trailing azalea (right) can be found growing from soil-filled crevices in the rock.

Opposite: The mountains of mid-Wales roll away to Cadair Idris in the North – seen from Plynlimon, source of the River Wye, the Severn and the Rheidol.

Life above 3,000 feet is tough. Rainfall is high and frosts are vicious. The constant winter wind is loaded with millions of tiny ice-crystals. Snow may cover the ground for up to six months of the year. In north-facing hollows on Scotland's highest mountains the snow only melts in exceptionally hot summers. The sun shines more brightly through the clear mountain air and the high level of ultra-violet light stunts plant growth. Trees rarely survive up here. Successful mountain plants are low-growing, hugging the ground and clinging on to rocks and thin soils to survive.

Many of our mountain plants also grow in the Arctic and the Alps. There are strange clubmosses, some like miniature fir trees, others sprawling and covered with bright yellow cones. Cushions of pink moss campion and white starry saxifrage grow by mountain springs. Miniature trailing azaleas creep over the rocks, which everywhere are blotched and patterned with lichens. The least willow copes with the problems of mountain life by keeping most of its twigs and branches underground. Its presence is only given away when a few leafy shoots appear and flower in summer.

Mid-week in November and the summits and shores of Wasdale are left to the sheep and the gulls. In summer the narrow lanes and fells of the Lake District are choked with holiday makers.

*T*hough not particularly high, it can still be a hard struggle to reach the top of Britain's mountains. The awaiting view and the feeling of freedom that comes from walking the ridges is worth all the effort – that's if the clouds don't descend and swamp the summit in a damp white shroud. Golden eagles quarter the hills in parts of Scotland and red deer appear on the skyline. Ptarmigan put on white winter plumage and mountain hares, invisible in their winter coats, leave ghostly footprints in the snow.

The mountainous regions of England and Wales have understandably become popular with millions of people otherwise confined to nearby towns. Snowdonia, the Pennines and the Cumbrian mountains are within easy reach of Manchester, Liverpool and Leeds. We value our uplands so highly as places of relaxation that the Lake District had to be sealed off from traffic one day in the summer of 1989. It was simply full up. Traffic was nose to tail down all of the major entrance roads.

The mountains of northwest Scotland are far less accessible, although old single-track roads are now quickly being replaced by faster highways. Skye, Applecross, Torridon, Foinaven are names that bring memories of spectacular mountain scenery to those that know these places. Stand on the Stoer Peninsular and to the south you can see mountain after mountain, each one distinct, rising out of the coastal plain: Canisp, Suilven, Stac Pollaidh, Cul More, once seen they are seldom forgotten.

Above: The Cairngorms and Loch Morlich. Ospreys bred and fished here before the tourist invasion. The mountains are breeding grounds for golden eagles, snow bunting, golden plover, dotterel, dunlin, peregrine falcons and many other birds.

Opposite: Winter in the Cairngorms – white hills and galeforce winds. A last snowy wilderness and Britain's largest nature reserve now threatened with further extensive skiing developments.

Britain's most famous mountains are suffering under the pressure of their popularity. Snowdon, the highest of the Welsh peaks at 3,559 feet, can now be climbed by simply sitting in a train. In the late 19th century, the Highland Railway and its branchlines opened up the Scottish mountains to wealthy sportsmen from the south. The Cairngorms became popular with skiers and in the 1950s plans were drawn up to develop the nearby village of Aviemore into an all-year tourist complex. The view of the mountains from Aviemore station has changed little since then but the village itself has grown beyond all recognition.

In the early days skiers had to walk a long way to reach the slopes but in 1960 a road was built to the foot of Cairn Gorm. Chairlifts and ski tows were added and new corries were opened up as demand for facilities increased. Now, weather permitting, you can always take a chairlift up to 3,600 feet, only a short walk and 484 feet away from the summit. People even bring their dogs with them on the lift. The four major peaks over 4,000 feet are easily reached from here. The high granite plateau, once protected from intrusion by its remoteness, is now explored by thousands of people all the year round.

Such developments bring prosperity to some people and pleasure to many more. But here in the Cairngorms they have also opened up one of the last places in Britain to escape exploitation. Skiers, hill walkers, plant collectors, birdwatchers and climbers are now joined by mountain bikers and the irritating noise of motorised tricycles. Ground-nesting birds like dotterel and golden plovers are disturbed. Crows and gulls, attracted to the mountains by food scraps and other litter, rob nests of eggs and chicks and the fragile mountain vegetation is slowly trampled to death. Soil erosion becomes a problem on paths, roads and ski slopes.

Developers want permission to extend skiing into unspoilt corries away from present developments. New roads and carparks, more chair lifts and restaurants would insure the demise of a landscape of great natural beauty. Wildlife would suffer and for many people the appeal of these remote mountains would be lost. Plans for expansion have so far been defeated. A balance needs to be maintained between the demands of the leisure industry, the needs of local people and the requirements of nature. Ever improving access to Britain's remote countryside eventually destroys the landscape most people come to enjoy.

Left:
A globeflower opens with the sun to reveal a fly that has spent the night in the shelter of its petals.

Below: Cattle grazing contentedly at the foot of the Cairngorms.

Without over-grazing and over-burning, drainage, reseeding, chemical fertilisers and pesticides, Britain's mountain pastures can once again be full of flowers – and much less expensive to maintain.

Opposite: The Cumbrian Mountains.

For centuries shaggy mountain cattle grazed Britain's upland pastures. Lonely hills and mountain passes are crossed by a network of ancient tracks once used by drovers taking their herds down to southern markets. The wild goats you occasionally see on remote mountains in Wales and Scotland are descendants of the medieval flocks which were once an important part of the upland economy.

Sheep farming came to dominate the hills from the late 18th century onwards. Between 1782 and 1854 Scotland suffered the notorious Highland Clearances. Ruthless landowners, lured by stories of great profit, confiscated the ancestral lands of many highland farmers and converted them to sheep ranches. Inhabitants were evicted, often by great violence, and villages were sacked.

Traditional mountain pasture that has escaped over-grazing by sheep contains many beautiful flowers. The golden globeflower grows on wet upland meadows and mountain ledges. Mountain pansies, violets, milkwort, vetches and daisies hide amongst the summer grass. The rare Snowdon lily, like a white crocus with purple veins, blooms in May on a few mountain ledges in Wales.

Some arctic-alpine species like mountain avens, with eight creamy white petals and a mass of golden stamens, and mountain everlasting, pale papery flowers with silver leaves, also grow at sea-level on the coast of northern Scotland. The flora is at its richest on limestone and basic soils. Rough acid pasture is often covered with thousands of heath spotted orchids in summer.

*B*are hillsides of close-cropped grass broken by rocky outcrops and the occasional rowan or thorn tree are characteristic of high ground all over Britain. Much of this open moorland has been with us since early settlers cleared the hills of trees over 3,000 years ago. Ancient stone circles aligned with the stars, burial chambers and brochs are scattered over our moors. Solitary trees, often growing from cracks in the rocks, are witness to the fact that, without grazing, many moors would again be wooded.

Parts of Caithness, Orkney, Shetland and the Outer Hebrides are natural tundra and have never had trees. Some woodland was killed long ago by the development of peat bog, but most of our moorland is the result of a long history of human management. The last fifty years have brought major changes in land use. Many moors have been ploughed and re-seeded. Some have even been converted to arable land. The widespread use of pesticides in the 1960s caused the death of many animals and birds of prey.

Moors are uncultivated areas of high ground below the tree limit but above the level of enclosed pasture and arable land. The result of forest clearance and grazing, these open hills bring visitors to Britain from all over the world. A great deal of public money has been wasted converting moorland to improved pasture and even arable land.

By far the largest loss of moorland is to commercial forestry. Britain imports a lot of timber and there is undeniably a need to grow some of it at home. But the pace of moorland conversion has been alarming and, although it has slowed, much more is planned. Even in our national parks land is regularly lost to forestry. For millions of people, open moorland offers the chance of freedom from the confines of modern life. We need to protect what is left. We will surely miss it when it's gone.

Often described as a wilderness, Dartmoor's open hills are in fact the result of thousands of years of human management.

Above: Stone row at Merrivale. Another similar row runs parallel to this about 50 feet away. Constructed some 4,000 years ago when Dartmoor was densely populated, the original function of these stones is unclear.

Four thousand years ago Dartmoor was densely populated. The hills are covered with the remains of ancient settlements, stone circles and burial chambers. Great rows of standing stones stride over the moors, the longest running for two miles. At Grimspound the remains of 24 round dwellings, known as hutcircles, are clearly visible inside a circular enclosure. Some 5,000 Bronze Age hutcircles are scattered over Dartmoor. Aerial photographs reveal low stone walls running for miles in parallel lines over southern Dartmoor. Roughly divided into fields, these prehistoric boundaries separated many square miles of moor into pasture and arable land. These "reaves" show that extensive moorland management was already well-established here thousands of years ago.

Dartmoor was designated a royal game reserve in the 11th century and for 200 years the high ground was under forest law. Cultivation was mostly restricted to surrounding lower ground, then known as the Commons of Devon. Most towns and villages around Dartmoor today date from Saxon and Medieval times. Nestling in the valleys, they prospered from the lucrative wooltrade and the tin industry. The hills are littered with spoil heaps of medieval tinners. Although land around abandoned farmsteads sometimes reveals the ridge and furrow patterning of medieval strip-farming, Dartmoor's vegetation has largely been determined by a long history of grazing. Plants that cannot stand regular close-cropping have been eliminated. Those that are unpalatable are dominant.

*P*redecessors of Dartmoor ponies were recorded in the Domesday Book. Used by miners and farmers, quarry workers and peat cutters, they have laboured long for mankind. Shetland ponies were introduced to Dartmoor at the beginning of this century. The resulting smaller cross-breeds were sent in their thousands down the coal mines of England and Wales. Modern farmers have little use for Dartmoor ponies. There are no subsidies on ponies as there are on sheep and less profit usually means less care. Severe weather often brings starvation and suffering to those ponies that remain. Interbreeding has made them less hardy. Overgrazing by sheep and cattle has left a shortage of food. With the exception of breeding mares, Dartmoor ponies are sold at markets around the moors. A few go for riding. Most end up as petfood. Surely they deserve better treatment after centuries of serving our needs.

Above: Hay Tor from Hound Tor, Distinctive jointed blocks of granite dominate the high ground over much of Dartmoor.

Dartmoor ponies
entertain summer
visitors to the moors
but in severe winters
they suffer badly from
exposure and
starvation.
Interbreeding with
Shetland ponies has
made them less
resistant to the
extremes of moorland
life.

Above and Far right: Estate owners and their gamekeepers have encouraged the growth of a continuous blanket of heather on Britain's moors. Trees and shrubs have been eradicated and birds of prey have been persecuted in the interests of game.

Right: A red grouse surveys his domain in the Grampians. Without the hunting interest, even more of our moors would be planted with conifers.

Patches of heather on Britain's open moors are home to the red grouse. In the nineteenth century grouse-shooting became fashionable amongst the rich. Owners of moorland estates, especially in the Pennines and the southeastern Scottish Highlands, increasingly dedicated themselves to fostering their favourite game bird.

Parliament still begins its summer vacation in August in time for the start of the grouse season on the "Glorious Twelfth". Burning had always played a small part in moorland management, where grazing was not enough to keep scrub under control. With the rapid expansion of grouse-shooting, moor-burning became a regular practice.

Red grouse chicks eat insects for the first few days of their lives, but from then on their diet consists mostly of heather. Heather is relatively resistant to fire and its natural lifespan of about thirty years can be prolonged by burning – just as the life of a tree is extended by coppicing. Rotational burning has created a continuous patchwork of heather at different stages of maturity over much of Britain's moorland. New growth is encouraged, ensuring a regular supply of young shoots for both sheep and grouse. Dead heather is removed, allowing the dense cover necessary to raise chicks successfully, without completely swamping them in a tangle of rank undergrowth.

Right & opposite: The grouse moors of North Yorkshire in late summer.

Below: Moor burning is often used to destroy rather than encourage heather today, producing coarse grassland for sheep. Combined with hill drainage this has encouraged the large-scale invasion of bracken.

An almost continuous blanket of heather covers 160 square miles of the North York Moors, making this the most extensive tract of open heather moorland in England. In August the higher treeless slopes are often entirely purple, as millions of flowers come into bloom. On a still day in late summer the air is full of the buzzing of countless bees.

Traditional management of heather for sheep and grouse involves considerable skill and sensitivity. Moors are burnt in late autumn or early spring, but only when the ground is wet enough to prevent damage to roots and to the peat around them. If the fire is too hot or burns for too long, it can destroy the surface layer of peat causing long-term loss of soil fertility.

Where grouse-shooting is no longer popular, old skills have been lost. Moor-burning today seldom prolongs the life of traditional moorland plants. Instead it tends to destroy them. On moors managed exclusively for sheep, frequent unseasonal burning has killed off most of the heather and encouraged the growth of rough grass. Greatly increasing stocking density has the same effect.

Over-burning, moorland drainage and the absence of grazing all encourage bracken. Cattle once limited invasion by grazing spring growth and trampling older plants. Now they are rarely a part of moorland farming. Bracken is spreading over the North York Moors at a rate of about 300 acres a year. Today's answer is, of course, the regular application of selective herbicides.

Over one third
of our upland
grasslands,
heaths and
blanket bogs
have been lost or
significantly
damaged since
1950.

Many of Britain's nature reserves are on the site of old quarries and pits. With sensitive treatment, they can become colourful rock gardens and water parks full of wildlife interest. Sadly most are used as rubbish dumps.

Opposite: China clay pit in Cornwall.

*F*or many centuries we have exploited the hidden wealth of our mountains and moorlands. Hillsides around the coalfields of South Wales are riddled with clusters of old pits and mineshafts. Moorland on Cornwall's Penwith Peninsula is today a place of quiet and emptiness. One hundred and fifty years ago this was one of the world's most important metal mining areas. Then these moors were filled with intense industrial activity and the sky was obscured by smoke and fumes belching out of hundreds of chimney stacks. The large mine complexes at Botallack and Levant still recall the industrial landscape of the past. Elsewhere only an occasional ruined engine house remains.

Modern extraction industries produce waste on a massive scale, like the giant slag heaps which dominate the Welsh coal mining valleys. Parts of the Cornish moors are now hidden beneath naked white hills of quartz sand. Often rippled and patterned like dunes in a desert, this is the waste product of the china clay industry. China clay is one of Britain's most valuable raw material exports. Eighty per cent goes to the paper industry to produce, among other things, the glossy paper used in magazines and books. The pharmaceutical industry is another major customer.

Stark spoil heaps and disused pits filled with strange turquoise pools are part of the cost of extraction in the rapidly expanding china clay industry. Much research has been done to find grasses that will grow in this virtually sterile environment. Results have been encouraging but the cost of change is high. Dust pollution remains a serious nuisance. For each ton of clay extracted there are seven tons of waste. Nonetheless old pits and quarries can provide valuable habitats for plants and animals banished from surrounding land by modern farming and forestry.

As an island nation we should be ultra proud of our coastline and the shallow sea around us, for they have provided Britain with a wealth of food and moated protection for at least eight thousand years.

Our forefathers who fished and gathered from our inshore waters understood their moods and rejoiced in their unending bounty. Only more recently have we begun to understand that estuaries and continental shelves are not there purely for our own convenience. They are the kidneys of the land, cleaning the muddied waters of natural erosion, and the ovaries of the ocean, providing a surfeit of nascent life, eggs and larvae spawning out to restock the open sea.

After more than 400 years of profligate misuse of this our most precious resource, we are at last beginning to come to our senses. Thanks to the stupendous effort of the National Trust's "Enterprise Neptune", more than 500 miles of our best remaining coastline is owned and managed by them.

Thanks to tireless campaigning by Greenpeace, F.O.E., the Marine Conservation Society and many others against continued pollution by every unthinkable and unsinkable product of our effluent society, positive changes are in the pipeline.

At last industry is beginning to clean up its act. Businesses are now making a profit from recycling waste and the cogeneration of energy – profit from doing things the right way. We have at last acknowledged the fact that long sea outfalls which are not backed up by efficient effluent treatment only deposit the sewage and its associated problems on the

From sink to resource, *a little bit of potty training*

floor of other parts of the marine ecosystem, and often on the bathing beaches of down-current authorities. Composting our sewage to produce organic soil conditioner is beginning to relieve the load and solve many other problems into the bargain. It all comes down to a bit of potty training.

The Thames, Tees and Tyne are once again living rivers and the North Sea oil industry has done a brilliant, though not untarnished, job. Yet there are many clouds on the marine horizon.

Fish farming is in essence a good idea which should have given the natural fish stocks a well deserved rest from over exploitation. Yet despite quotas, over-fishing appears to be the dis-order of the E.E.C.. Meanwhile, off the shelf fish farms providing quick returns have grotesquely polluted otherwise untouched sea lochs in some very insidious and damaging ways. At the same time overproduction has drastically reduced the price of the end product, slashing profit margins and pointing to bankruptcy. Who will clean up the mess after that?

Then there is the sad fact that every one of our estuaries is also threatened with plans to construct a barrage or marina, and usually both. The arguments generally go something like this: clean green energy from tidal power, lots of jobs, and the boaties (and I am one of them) have an equal right to make use of the waters... But so do the birds and the fish and the crabs and the lobsters, the shrimps, worms, whelks, winkles and all the other members of the marine food chain which service the kidneys of the land and the ovaries of the ocean. DB

T he coastline is Britain's most spectacular natural feature. Over 6,000 miles of constant change and diversity. From the soaring, wave-battered cliffs of Land's End to the sand dunes of Cardigan Bay; from the rocks, lochs and islands of the northwest coast of Scotland to the mile-wide sandflats of East Anglia – our rich coastal heritage has a wide variety of dramatic scenery and provides a huge range of habitats for wildlife.

Britain's shape is always changing in an endless process of loss and gain. Where the rock is soft, the cliffs are eroded and the sea smooths the coast into straight lines and gentle curves. Where the rock is more resistant, vertical cliffs tower above the sea, forming prominent headlands and sheltered coves. Eroded material is carried along the shore and deposited on shingle banks and sandy beaches.

Mud and sand accumulate at the mouths of

The varied landscape
of Britain's coastline.
Opposite: Cattle on
the pale sands of
Balnakeil Bay.
Left: Sea-bird colony
on Handa Island.
Below: Unstable chalky
cliffs cut into the
Purbeck Hills.

rivers. Estuaries gradually silt up and old harbours become landlocked. The volume of the Mersey continues to fall despite a massive programme of dredging. Rivers that once flowed directly into the sea, now discharge into hundreds of creeks meandering through salt marshes and growing mudflats. Many thousands of acres have been added to Britain this way.

Sea-level, too, rises and falls according to the amount of ice on the polar caps. For the last 750 years the sea has been gradually rising. Whole towns have tumbled over the cliffs and been lost to the waves. The "greenhouse effect" speeds up the process – as gases like methane and carbon dioxide build up in the atmosphere, the planet warms up, the polar ice caps melt more quickly and sea level rises. The land itself also tilts and bends. The English coast is presently sinking, while Scotland is slowly rising. Land around the Thames estuary is dropping by one foot every 100 years.

Billions of pebbles are carried along Britain's coast in the sea. Thrown up by the waves, they form steep terraced banks, fringing beaches and long spits. Shingle beaches border 25 per cent of the British coastline, but only occasionally are conditions right for colonisation by plants. Open to the full force of the sea and constantly in motion, shingle is usually too unstable to support plantlife.

Ridges formed in severe storms, above all but the highest tides, however, do offer the right conditions for growth. Here blue-flowered oysterplants and purple sea peas cling to the shingle above the drift line. Horned poppies form untidy colonies where the ground is most stable. Sea kale produces a huge rosette of blue-green leaves and a mass of white flowers in summer. A single plant may be more than three feet across, quite an achievement in such a harsh environment.

Colonisers of the storm-piled pebble slopes must also cope with extreme changes in temperature. Water quickly drains away through the pebbles and there are few available nutrients. Plants adapted to life on exposed shingle ridges have very long roots, both to anchor themselves to their mobile home and to reach deep into the shingle for water and food. They depend for their survival on the meagre amount of soil trapped between the pebbles.

Chesil Beach is a shingle ridge running for nearly eighteen miles down the Dorset coast. Joining the Isle of Portland to the mainland, it encloses a brackish lagoon, cut off from the sea except for a small opening into Portland Harbour. Britain's only nesting colony of mute swans has lived here since the 11th century, when monks first reared them for meat. The leeward side of Chesil Beach is remarkable for the variety of plantlife it supports.

Horned poppies in the lee of the shingle ridge at Blakeney Point, Norfolk.
Opposite: Exposed to the constant movement of the ocean, the beach at Worbarrow Bay is too unstable to support plantlife.

Building breakwaters, seawalls and groynes upsets the natural dynamics of the changing shoreline.
Opposite: Shingle has accumulated on Chesil Beach for nearly fourteen thousand years. Now the ridge is starting to erode.
Above: Harbour wall at Mullion.
Right: Away from trampling feet, sea peas help stabilise shingle above the drift-line.

Mankind has fought a constant battle against the sea's powers of erosion and accretion. It soon became obvious that to defend one place often meant sacrificing another. Building a seawall to prevent one harbour from silting up or becoming trapped behind a shingle spit, often caused the demise of a rival port further along the coast.

Shingle ridges are important as sea defences. Building artificial breakwaters, groynes, seawalls and even promenades upsets the natural balance of loss and gain. Shingle features are dependent upon a constant supply of pebbles. Chesil Beach has probably been forming since the end of the last glaciation. Today it receives little new shingle. It has ceased to grow and is eroding in places. Property in its shelter is increasingly at risk.

The nuclear power station at Dungeness was unwisely built on a shingle beach. Continuous traffic is destroying the ridge system. Lorries must constantly feed the beach with pebbles in order to prevent disaster. Beaches elsewhere are inevitably suffering as a result. The most significant threat to our shingle beaches is the extraction of gravel for the construction industry, both from the coastline and from offshore deposits.

Shingle plantlife is very vulnerable to trampling. Ground-nesting birds like ringed plovers and terns are also at risk from disturbance. Ten sites around the British coast are now protected for their wildlife value. It is sometimes necessary to limit access in the breeding season and fence off particularly sensitive vegetation. It is important to realise that many species are unlikely to survive in Britain without this sort of protection.

Right: Sand dunes covered with flowers and orchid-filled marshy hollows are preserved on the nature reserve at Kenfig Burrows. Next door is the heavy industry of Port Talbot. *Below:* Coastal dunes in the far north of Scotland are spared the stress of the summer tourist invasion further south.

With the tide out, beaches dry up and the wind blows the sand inshore. Above the high-tide mark, various grasses and plants like sea holly and sea bindweed are able to grow on the accumulating sand. They in turn trap more sand and dunes gradually form. Marram grass is by far the most efficient stabiliser of sand dunes. Once it is well-established, mosses and lichens are able to colonise the bare sand between the tufts of grass.

Wet "slacks" develop in the lee of the dunes and support a rich variety of wildlife. Marsh helleborine, marsh orchids and the rare natterjack toad thrive here. Common fleabane is often abundant. Its yellow daisies attract shimmering red and black burnet moths. Sand dunes once provided important grazing for coastal farms. From the Middle Ages onwards they were often used as commercial rabbit warrens. Ancient villages lost to the advancing sand now lie buried beneath the dunes. The village of Forvie on the east coast of Scotland, north of Aberdeen, was

abandoned in 1413 after 1500 years of settlement.

In Scotland sand dunes are still important for grazing cattle and sheep. In England and Wales they are now mainly used for recreation. Uncontrolled trampling, horse-riding, fire-lighting, car rallying and motorbike scrambling around popular resorts has destroyed the delicate binding vegetation, resulting in large-scale damage to the dunes. Dunes are a first line of defence against the sea. Neglecting them could bring disaster in exceptionally bad weather. In some places dunes are now treated as rubbish tips.

Wildlife is best encouraged by replanting eroded dunes with marram grass and restricting access in sensitive areas to boardwalks. Light grazing maintains the greatest diversity of plant species on stable dunes by limiting the growth of scrub. Without grazing, dense thickets of sea buckthorn develop. Sand dunes, like shingle beaches, are part of the coastal system of loss and gain. Stabilising one region can starve another of sand.

Britain's estuaries have a long history of human settlement. Land reclamation, ports, industrial and urban expansion and now, marina mania, have greatly reduced and degraded our estuarine mudflats and saltmarshes.
Right: Sea lavender no longer blooms in plenty on our tidal marshes.

Continuously supplied with nutrients from rivers and the sea, estuaries are one of the earth's most productive natural environments. Enormous numbers of molluscs, crustaceans and worms live on the fertile mudflats. Otters are attracted to estuaries by the huge shoals of fish in their teeming waters. Many millions of wintering birds feed on the flats and at the water's edge. Millions more recuperate on the marshes on their migration journeys. The world's largest herd of common seals, some 6,000 animals is found in the Wash on the east coast of England.

Many specialised plants grow abundantly on the salt marshes. Adapted to life on the tidal edge, they can even survive long periods of submersion in seawater when the tide is in. Carpets of eel grass and fleshy glasswort are peppered with the tiny pink or white flowers of sea spurrey. In July saltmarshes are often covered with a pale purple haze as sea lavender comes into bloom. The colour continues into late summer, when sea astors, looking like Michaelmas daisies, begin to flower.

Alien species and diseases, often imported with stock for shellfish farms, have had a devastating effect on estuarine life. Oyster drills, slipper limpets, American clams and Japanese seaweed have now become a serious nuisance on Britain's shores. The introduction of an American saltmarsh grass produced a vigorous hybrid, rice grass, which has now been widely planted to speed up land "reclamation". It quickly covers the mudflats to the exclusion of all other plants — yet another monoculture of modern farming.

Britain's estuaries have been much abused in the last one hundred years. Huge areas of saltmarsh have been converted to agricultural land. Ports, marinas, urban and industrial complexes are constantly expanding. Estuaries have been dredged for navigation and "in-filled" with domestic and industrial waste. Nearly fifty per cent of the estuaries of England and Wales are poisoned with sewage, oil, pesticides, fertilisers and toxic industrial discharges. Shellfish are unfit to eat. Seals are dying. Commercial fishing is suffering. Bathers are at risk.

S heep and cattle have long grazed Britain's windy cliff-top pastures. Where this practice continues, carpets of pale blue spring squill and colonies of tiny green-winged orchids are frequently found on the short turf. The Lizard Peninsula in Cornwall is internationally famous for its coastal grasslands. Conservationists once sought to protect them by excluding livestock. Gorse and rough grasses were quick to smother rare and more delicate species.

Local people, remembering summer picnics on cliff-top pasture full of wildflowers, knew that grazing had always been important to these rich grasslands. Learning how different plants respond to grazing now enables us to encourage individual species by controlling grazing pressure. Walkers often object to sharing coastal footpaths with cattle, but livestock play a vital part in maintaining the open grasslands we come to enjoy. However, it is essential that grazing remains light. Modern intensive methods soon destroy ancient flower-filled pastures.

A long tradition of grazing sheep at the water's edge has produced large areas of dense fescue turf. In early summer the sea washes around emerald green cushions crowned with pink thrift. This beautiful flower flourishes almost everywhere on the British coast. Coastal grasslands are vital feeding grounds for millions of geese, swans and ducks like widgeon and pintail. Much reduced by coastal development and land reclamation, our coastal grasslands are even plundered for sale in garden centres as "sea-washed turf".

Above: Carpets of pale blue spring squill and delicate green-winged orchids grow on cliffs where light grazing limits rough grasses and scrub.
Left: White flowering scurvy grass, rich in vitamin C, and glossy sea beet on the Lizard's clifftop pasture.

Opposite top: The sea carrot, known as Queen Anne's Lace, grows on grassy cliffs in the South.
Opposite below: The difference in vegetation at the cliff edge, on the path and inside the army range on Flowers Barrow, Dorset. Grazing is minimal and the long summer grass is still full of butterflies.

Long-distance footpaths around Britain's coast pass by hundreds of miles of sheer cliffs. Crumbling grey slates and shales, pale granite veined with quartz, pure chalk, red and green serpentine streaked with white talc, and stratified cliffs, sheered and contorted by movements of the earth – as the rock changes, so does the scenery. The cliffed coastline is a dramatic record of millions of years of the earth's history.

Some of our most spectacular cliffs are home to great colonies of seabirds. Just below Cape Wrath, in the far north west of Scotland, is Handa Island. Its red sandstone cliffs have weathered into hundreds of crevices and ledges. A huge stack, nearly 400 feet high, has broken away from the cliff. In summer the din of over 100,000 nesting birds is incredible. This isolated, weather-beaten island is now managed by the RSPB.

Guillemots and razorbills stand, densely packed, on the ledges. Kittiwakes and fulmars wheel around the cliffs and fit in where they can. Puffins whir by, surprisingly agile on their stubby wings. Skuas patrol the island looking for food. But everything is not as it should be. Sand eels are the staple diet of breeding seabirds. Abundant in the 1960s and 70s due to over-fishing of their predators, herring and mackerel, sand eels are now themselves being fished.

Sand eels are reduced to "marine oil" used in products like margarine, and turned into fish meal for chickens and pigs. Buying these products, we are contributing to the decline of our seabird population. Catches of sand eels have been falling since 1982. There was almost total breeding failure amongst the terns, kittiwakes, puffins and skuas in Shetland in 1988. Fishing for sand eels is growing in feeding grounds around Handa, threatening one of Scotland's most important sites for seabirds.

Over-fishing of Britain's coastal waters is leading to breeding failure in our great sea-bird colonies.

Opposite and below: Handa Island, R.S.P.B. reserve.
Above: Engine house of a nineteenth century Cornish tin mine on sheer cliffs at Botallack.

Above top: Cushions of thrift can be found almost everywhere along Britain's coast. *Above:* Tree mallow. These strange plants may reach ten feet tall. *Right:* Hairy lichen covering rocks on the Lizard, a sure sign that the air is still relatively unpolluted.

Where cliffs are resistant to the pounding waves, salt-sprayed rocks and ledges are often a mass of flowers in summer. White sea campion and roseroot, woolly kidney vetch, cushions of thrift and sky-blue sheep's-bit grow in abundance. Colonies of tree mallow, with velvety leaves and gnarled woody stems, produce hundreds of rich purple flowers. Three-cornered leeks, with clusters of white bells on strange triangular stems, grow by red valerian. Even bluebells thrive on cliffs in the west.

Escaped garden flowers, like deep orange montbretia, monopolise some cliffs in the south. The thick fleshy leaves and yellow star-like flowers of the hottentot fig now swamp parts of the Lizard.

They look beautiful but, as they gradually colonise the coast, they displace rare and fragile native species, destroying habitats and starving wildlife of food. Planted to brighten up the countryside, alien species can become a serious nuisance.

The bizarre metamorphic rocks of Lizard Head and the hard granites of Penwith are seldom visible. The colour of the cliffs comes from lichens living on the surface of the rock. The fresh Atlantic winds are relatively unpolluted and lichens grow everywhere. Soaring stable cliffs are an irresistible challenge to climbers. Today it is common to clear the cliff face of plants and debris before attempting the climb. It's a far greater challenge to scale the cliff and leave no sign of your presence.

Left: Red valerian, probably a foreign introduction, grows on cliffs and old stone walls throughout Britain.
Right: Sea campion.
Below: Where cliffs are stable and protected from grazing, scrub and woodland develops.

Plants on Britain's boulder-strewn beaches grow in distinct bands across the shore according to their relative needs. Lichens paint a black stripe across the top of the beach. Green seaweeds grow in permanent rockpools veneered with red seaweeds. Rocks lower down the shore are festooned with brown seaweeds. These are also graded down the beach and are easily recognised from their names. Channelled wrack and twisted wrack give way to bladderwrack and egg wrack. Toothed wrack comes next, then it, too, is replaced by giant oarweeds. Rocks below the tide line are encrusted with barnacles, limpets, whelks and mussels. Sea anemones, shore crabs, shrimps and starfish – marine life is obvious and plentiful on healthy rocky beaches.

Below: A slippery mass of seaweed clings to the rocks along Britain's shoreline. Sea anemones, shellfish, crabs, shrimps and starfish are abundant.

Left: Looking across the rocky shore of northwest Scotland towards the Isle of Skye. A bridge is soon to replace the ferry linking Skye to the mainland. Major commercial development is bound to follow.

L ife on Britain's sandy beaches can be difficult to spot. Billions of microscopic algae live amongst the grains of sand. Starfish live in the sand below the low water mark. Empty shells on the strand line are evidence of the many invertebrates living beneath the surface of the beach. Cockles and razor shells, clams and Venus shells burrow out of sight when the tide goes out.

Ripples left on the sand by the retreating waves are covered with little depressions and coiled pyramids of sand, betraying the presence of lugworms. Hundreds of delicate sandy tubes made by trumpet worms and sand mason are stranded with the shells at the top of the beach. Far fewer shells are washed up on our beaches today. This is often a direct result of chemical pollution.

Opposite and left: Sandymouth Bay, emptied of visitors at nightfall.
Below: Gruinard Bay. Gruinard Island was used during the Second World War for experiments with germ warfare. It's still contaminated with anthrax and out of bounds to the public.

Millions of people are understandably drawn to Britain's sandy beaches in the holiday season and wildlife is suffering as a result. Sewage facilities at resorts are often inadequate to deal with the huge influx of tourists.

Right: A fish farm in the distance on Loch Torridon. There is hardly a sea loch on the west coast of Scotland, around Skye and the Western Isles that doesn't contain caged fish.

The west coast of Scotland is wonderfully convoluted. The sea often runs far into the mountains. River valleys, deepened by glaciers, were flooded as the ice gradually melted and the sea began to rise. The resulting sea-lochs have a powerful, tranquil beauty. Loch Torridon is crystal-clear. Carpets of seaweed are clearly visible through the reflection of the mountains on the water's surface. Mountain goats graze the seaweed on the shores of Loch Linnhe, which carries the sea to the foot of Ben Nevis, and into Loch Leven below the misty summits of Glencoe. Thousands of jelly fish gather in Loch Hourn. Otters are commonly seen fishing and playing at the water's edge. Scotland's sea-lochs are full of wildlife, long gone from southern estuaries.

Fish and seafood are plentiful but methods of harvesting fish are changing. Sea-lochs are now commonly the site of caged fish farms. Intensive fish-farming has a far-reaching, detrimental effect on the environment. A large farm produces as much waste as the sewage from a village of several hundred people. Untreated waste washes directly into the sea. Densely packed, farmed fish are prone to disease and infect wild populations. Cages are sprayed with antibiotics and fungicides. Escaped fish reproduce with their wild counterparts and the gene-stock of our native fish is corrupted. Otters and seals, attracted to the huge numbers of fish, are persecuted for damaging the cages. Herons, too, are slaughtered in their hundreds for taking the fish.

On the west coast of Scotland, around the Isle of Skye and the Western Isles there is hardly a sea loch that does not contain cages packed with Atlantic salmon. The Highlands and Islands Development Board and the EEC cover seventy per cent of the cost of setting up fish farms. Around half of the production is in the hands of just three companies. They may bring welcome employment to remote regions but it is scandalous that there are no effective controls over emissions. Unwanted fish from farms are regularly used to restock rivers. Salmon and trout are becoming cheaper at great cost to the natural environment.

All our estuaries
are threatened
by pollution,
barrages,
marinas and
other
commercial
developments.

Right: In the summer of 1990, after a week's intensive cleaning, remote beaches on Bigbury Bay in Devon are still badly polluted. The air stinks of oil and dispersants. Oil ran up the estuary of the River Erme, until then relatively unspoilt.
Left: The southeast coast.

Some of Britain's beaches are in a disgusting state. Sewage, pumped into the sea just off the coast, washes back onto the shore. Everything that goes down the drain comes back in the surf. The drift line is littered with the indestructible refuse of modern life, dumped offshore and returned by the tides. Millions of people now have the time and money to visit the coast. Sewage facilities are often inadequate to cope with the huge influx of tourists and the rapid expansion of resorts.

On the east coast in particular, thousands of seabirds, fish and seals are dying, poisoned by toxic waste and coated with oil. Dispersant sprays used to clean up oil spillages might offer short-term relief to wildlife but they cause longer-lasting harm to the environment than the oil itself. Radioactive waste from coastal powerstations is causing great public concern. Over-exploitation by massive factory ships has made the fishing industry little more than a memory in many small harbour towns.

In 1963, the National Trust appealed for money to purchase stretches of unspoilt coast in England, Wales and Northern Ireland. By 1984, half of the targeted 900 miles were under their protection. Pressure for development on the remaining land had become so intense that "Enterprise Neptune" was relaunched. To date the National Trust have raised 14 million pounds by public donation and 514 miles of coastline have been purchased. Raising money this way, we can protect the coastline from some of the sad consequences of unbridled commercial development.

In 1976 Britain was asked by the EEC to list its bathing beaches. This was part of a European drive to clean up the coast and guarantee safe bathing at resorts. The British government only designated 27 beaches, compared to 1,498 listed in France and 3,308 listed in Italy! Public outcry forced the government to designate 392 bathing beaches in 1987. Forty per cent of the beaches listed subsequently failed to meet the European standard.

*T*he landscape is a reflection of your lifestyle. What will you leave behind for your children?

The choice is yours

National Agencies

Ark
498 Harrow Road
London W9 3QA

British Trust for Conservation Volunteers
2 Mandela Street
London NW1 0DU

Conservation Foundation
1 Kensington Gore
London SW7 2AR

Council for the Protection of Rural England
Warwick House
25-27 Buckingham Palace Road
London SW1W 0PP

Friends of the Earth
26-28 Underwood Street
London N1 7JU

Forestry Commission
231 Corstorphine Road
Edinburgh EH12 7AT

Gaia
Coombe Mill
St Giles on the Heath
Launceston
Cornwall PL15 9OY

Greenpeace UK
30-31 Islington Green
London N1 8XE

Marine Conservation Society
4 Gloucester Road
Ross-on-Wye
Herefordshire HR9 5BU

National Society for Clean Air
136 North Street
Brighton BN1 1RG

National Trust
42 Queen Anne's Gate
London SW1H 9AS

National Trust for Scotland
5 Charlotte Square
Edinburgh EH2 4DR

Nature Conservancy Council
Northminster House
Peterborough PE1 1VA

Royal Society for Nature Conservation
The Green, Nettleham
Lincoln LN2 2NR

Royal Society for the Protection of Birds
The Lodge
Sandy
Bedfordshire SG19 2DL

Scottish Wildlife Trust
25 Johnston Terrace
Edinburgh EH1 2NH

Soil Association
80 Colston Street
Bristol BS1 5BB

The Woodland Trust
Autumn Park
Dysart Road
Grantham
Lincolnshire NG31 6LL

The Woodland Trust for Scotland
54 Manor Place
Edinburgh EH3 7EH

World Wide Fund for Nature
Panda House, Wayside Park
Godalming
Surrey GU7 1XR

Local Agencies

Avon Wildlife Trust
The Old Police Station
32 Jacob's Wells Road
Bristol BS8 1DR

Bedfordshire and Huntingdonshire Wildlife Trust
Priory Country Park
Barkers Lane
Bedford MK41 9SH

Berkshire, Buckinghamshire and Oxfordshire Naturalists' Trust
3 Church Cowley Road
Rose Hill
Oxford OX4 3JR

Brecknock Wildlife Trust
Lion House
7 Lion Street
Brecon
Powys LD3 7AY

Cambridgeshire Wildlife Trust
5 Fulbourn Manor
Manor Walk
Fulbourn
Cambridge CB1 5BN

Cheshire Conservation Trust
c/o Marbury Country Park
Northwich
Cheshire CW9 6AT

Cleveland Wildlife Trust
The Old Town Hall
Mandale Road
Thornaby
Cleveland TS17 6AW

Cornwall Trust for Nature Conservation
Dairy Cottage
Trelissick
Truro
Cornwall TR3 6QL

Cumbria Trust for Nature Conservation
Church Street
Ambleside
Cumbria LA22 0BU

Derbyshire Wildlife Trust
Elvaston Country Park
Derby DE7 3EP

Devon Wildlife Trust
35 New Bridge Street
Exeter
Devon EX4 3AH

Dorset Trust for Nature Conservation
39 Christchurch Road
Bournemouth BH1 3NS

Durham Wildlife Trust
Old Elvet
Durham DH1 3HN

Dyfed Wildlife Trust
7 Market Street
Haverford West
Dyfed SA61 1NF

Essex Naturalists Trust
Fingringhoe Wick Nature
Reserve
Fingringhoe
Colchester
Essex CO5 7DN

Glamorgan Wildlife Trust
Nature Centre
Fountain Road
Tondu
Mid Glamorgan CF32 0EH

Gloucester Trust for Nature Conservation
Church House
Standish
Stonehouse GL10 3EU

Gwent Wildlife Trust
16 White Swan Court
Church Street
Monmouth
Gwent NP5 3BR

Hampshire and Isle of Wight Naturalists Trust
8 Market Place
Romsey
Hampshire SO5 8NB

Herefordshire Nature Trust
Community House
25 Castle Street
Hereford HR1 2NW

Hertfordshire and Middlesex Wildlife Trust
Grebe House
St. Michael's Street
St. Albans
Hertfordshire AL3 4SN

Kent Trust for Nature Conservation
The Annexe
La Bower Mount Road
Maidstone
Kent ME16 8AX

Lancashire Trust for Nature Conservation
The Pavilion
Cuerdon Park Wildlife Centre
Bamber Bridge
Preston
Lancashire PR5 6AU

Leicestershire and Rutland Trust for Nature Conservation
1 West Street
Leicester LE1 6UU

Lincolnshire and South Humberside Trust for Nature Conservation
The Manor House
Alford
Lincolnshire LN13 9DL

London Wildlife Trust
80 York Way
London N1 9AG

Manx Nature Conservation Trust
Ballamoar House
Ballaugh
Isle of Man

Montgomery Trust for Nature Conservation
8 Severn Square
Newtown
Powys SY16 2AG

Norfolk Naturalists' Trust
72 Cathedral Close
Norwich
Norfolk NR1 4DF

Northamptonshire Wildlife Trust
Lings House
Billing Lings
Northampton NN3 4BE

Northumberland Wildlife Trust
c/o Hanock Museum
Barras Bridge
Newcastle upon Tyne
NE2 4PT

North Wales Naturalists' Trust
376 High Street
Bangor Gwynedd LL57 1YE

Nottinghamshire Wildlife Trust
310 Sneiton Dale
Nottingham NG3 7DN

Radnorshire Wildlife Trust
1 Gwalia Annaxe
Lthon Road
Llandrindod Wells
Powys LD1 6AS

Shropshire Trust for Nature Conservation
St. George's Primary School
Frankwell
Shrewsbury SY3 8JP

Somerset Trust for Nature Conservation
Fyne Court
Broomfield
Bridgwater TA5 2EQ

Staffordshire Nature Conservation Trust
Coutts House
Sandon
Staffordshire ST18 0DN

Suffolk Wildlife Trust
Park Cottage
Saxmundham
Suffolk IP17 1DQ

Surrey Wildlife Trust
Hatchlands
East Clandon
Guildford GU4 7RT

Sussex Wildlife Trust
Woods Mill
Henfield
West Sussex BN5 9SD

Urban Wildlife Trust
131-133 Sherlock Street
Birmingham B5 6NB

Warwickshire Nature Conservation Trust
Montague Road
Warwick CV34 5LW

Wiltshire Trust for Nature Conservation
19 High Street
Devizes
Wiltshire SN10 1AT

Worcestershire Nature Conservation Trust
Hanbury Road
Droitwich
Worcestershire WR9 7DU

Yorkshire Wildlife Trust
3rd Floor
10 Toft Green
York YO1 1JT

Index